Entrepreneurship in Africa

The Spiritual Dimension

Published by
Adonis & Abbey Publishers Ltd
P. O. Box 43418
London
SE11 4XZ
http://www.adonis-abbey.com
Email: editor@adonis-abbey.com

First Edition, February 2010

Copyright 2010 © Stewart Chibanda

British Library Cataloguing-in-Publication Data
A catalogue record for this book is available from the British Library

ISBN:9781906704636

The moral right of the author has been asserted

All rights reserved. No part of this book may be reproduced, stored in a retrieval system or transmitted at any time or by any means without the prior permission of the publisher

Layout Artist/Technical Editor, Jan B. Mwesigwa

Printed and bound in Great Britain

Entrepreneurship in Africa

The Spiritual Dimension

By

Stewart Chibanda

Special Dedication

This book is dedicated to my late father Bruce Chibanda and mother Maudy Madzimbamuto Chibanda.

These were very special people to me. There are some people in life whose greatness is not easily noticed, it only takes confirmation from those close to them. This is how I see my parents and I can confirm that they were great individuals. I am sure my brothers and sisters will agree with me on that. My dad was a charming man and my mother was outspoken and full of advice. Mum and dad, I miss you so much. You were a blessing in our lives and I thank God for having known you. I cannot turn back the hands of time but live on the sweet memories of the good times I had with you.

Great Thanks

I thank God for having found favour in His eyes, in allowing me to write this book.

Many Thanks

Many thanks go to my wife and children and all my friends and pastors who have supported me in different ways.

CONTENTS

Special dedication v
Contents vi
Introduction ix

Chapter 1
Have a vision 1

Chapter 2
Training for success 11

Chapter 3
The Power of positive thinking 27

Chapter 4
Positive thinking – The Good Samaritan 33

Chapter 5
What is money? 37

Chapter 6
Spiritual Dimension of Entrepreneurship 41

Chapter 7
What is sin? 47

Chapter 8
Well Balanced Goals – Balanced Diet 51

Chapter 9
Gossip and Time Wasting 57

Chapter 10
Weak Link in the organization 63

Chapter 11
The Big Picture 65

Chapter 12
Expand your means..69

Chapter 13
Benchmarking..71

Chapter 14
Worrying and Sorrow 77

Chapter 15
Learn to see opportunities..81

Chapter 16
Rebuke mediocrity...89

Chapter 17
Transformation a must...91

Chapter 18
Humility Pays 95

Chapter 19
Man looks on the outside...99

Chapter 20
God Has A Plan For You...101

Chapter 21
Background of Suffering 107

Chapter 22
You can't be everybody's Friend 111

Chapter 23
Sacrifice 113

Chapter 24
Life is like a paradox 117

Chapter 25
As busy as a bee...119

Chapter 26
Who will teach our children?..123

Chapter 27
Beware of "first" customers or clients..125

Chapter 28
Personal Audit 127

Chapter 29
Celebrate your victory in advance 131

Chapter 30
Rich Sayings 133

Index 136

INTRODUCTION

Entrepreneurship is a journey, you don't arrive. You learn as you travel. That is why it is important to be futuristic.

This book is about how the mindset and attitude towards situations affect our enterprises. Many people want to start their own businesses or progress to great heights in their already established enterprises. The question is why don't they? This is what this book seeks to answer.

There is a gap that this book seeks to fill. It does this by exploring the spiritual dimension to entrepreneurship that is most of the time neglected. The strongholds that are often talked about are in the mind rather than out there. We all need positive internal dialogues.

It is a must read for all prospective and existing entrepreneurs. Faith is very important for our growth, faith in God and our capabilities. We all have the ability to create successful businesses, we have creation in us.

There are great benefits to be derived from this book. First and foremost is the realization of the power of God in our lives and how we can release those innate abilities He has given us. There are people who have gone before us, let us learn from them. You will see the importance of having not just a vision but an unshakable vision. You will be able to turn negative situations to positive ones if you only master the concepts in this book. This works for good for your enterprise.

Technical concepts have been simplified and made easy and interesting to read. The most amazing discovery is that entrepreneurship is not intricate but multi-faceted.

I have a dream, an African dream, a colourful dream, of a time when Africa will no longer be a perpetual recipient of donor aid, but a lender to other nations. You cannot give what you do not have. I look forward to a time when Africa will be able to add value to its raw materials. Africa should have its own vision, a uniting vision. Where there are two or more competing visions it becomes a division. As long as we have too many visions we will remain divided.

You can become a successful entrepreneur if you are willing to get some tips. Enjoy, as you read along.

Chapter 1

HAVE A VISION

vision is a mental image or picture you hold or the manner in which one sees or conceives of something. It is a dream. It is an image of a better future.

It is imperative that you set a vision for your business and hold on to it. Vision-setting is the starting point of any business. Your vision should direct you purposefully and motivate you. A vision is futuristic. It is the first step in developing your strategic plan.

Helen Keller said "It is a terrible thing to see and have no vision"

You should know what you want in the future. You should see the unseen, feel the unfelt, as if you have already achieved it. Some people will think you are over ambitious when they get to know your vision.

As an entrepreneur the vision guides you in your day-to-day decision making. You should be able to ask yourself at any point in time: '..is this course of action in line with the entity's vision?' It should be a shared vision. That is the only way it can be successfully realized. The head of the organization should act in line with the shared vision in his or her daily conduct. This includes being sensitive in awarding of perks in an organization.

It is amazing how enterprises in the U.S.A. still want to give out huge bonus perks to top management amidst the turmoil and recovery of the global financial crisis. If this is so, it can put the shared vision into jeopardy.

A vision is what you will be **tomorrow,** a mission is what you are **today**. A vision is what the enterprise would like to become while a mission describes what the entity is now. A vision statement usually start as follows 'to be a ………', 'to become the ………', 'to………'

On the other hand a a mission statement starts with 'we are..........', 'we at ....', 'we proclaim.......'

It has been observed that one of the reasons people fail to realise their vision is that they fail to break it down into actionable pieces or steps called strategies. Break it down into goals and action plans; who is going to do what and when? A vision is futuristic it cannot be achieved overnight or at one go. If you try to achieve the vision with haste it might end up de-motivating you. (Habakkuk 2: 2) says

> "Then the Lord answered me and said: 'Write the vision and make it plain on tablets. That he may run who reads it.'

It is important that you write down your vision on a piece of paper or your computer. Read it on a regular basis, meditate on it and say to yourself daily 'I can do all things through Christ who strengthens me.'

Relationship between Vision, Mission and Objectives

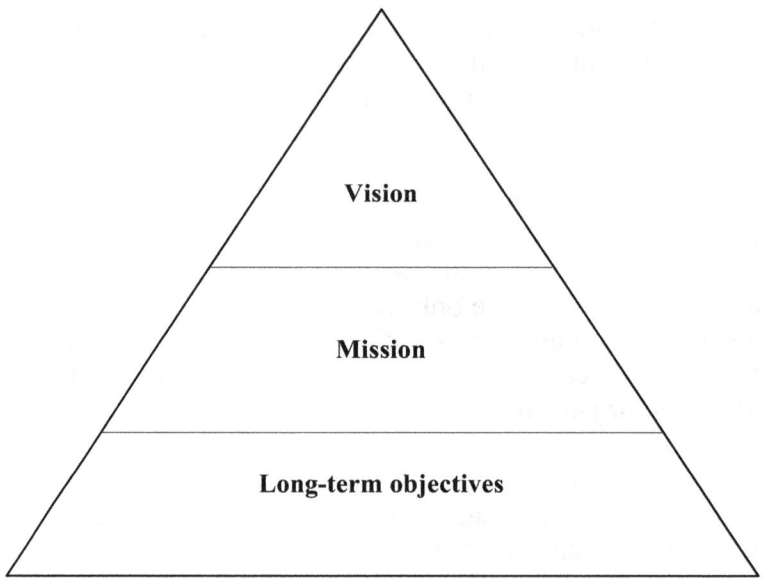

Run with the vision. When you come up with a vision be involved in its fulfilment. Remember no involvement, no commitment. At first don't delegate the vision too much. This is because not everyone is seeing what you are seeing. Therefore it takes time for people to buy into the vision. (Proverbs 29: 18) says:

> Where there is no vision, the people perish.

Let us seek divine guidance as we pursue our vision. God is supreme. When you seek guidance from God you automatically have a supernatural advantage over your peers and enemies. When God leads, something has to happen, he will lead in a manner that is best for you. God led the children of Israel out of Egypt. The scripture in (Exodus 13: 17) says:

> Then it came to pass, when Pharaoh had let the people go, that God did not lead them by way of the land of the Philistines, though that was shorter. God said 'Lest perhaps the people change their minds when they see war, and return to Egypt.'

Sometimes we want to use short cuts and most of the time short cuts glare at us in the face. Let God lead the way. He knows the route your vision should take. It only happens when you seek His divine intervention. The scripture in (Exodus 14: 19-20) records:

> And the Angel of God, who went before the camp of Israel, moved and went behind them; and the pillar of cloud went from before them and stood behind them. So it came between the camp of the Egyptians and the camp of Israel. Thus it was a cloud and darkness to the one, and it gave light by night to the other, so that the one did not come near the other all that night.

The Israelites had a supernatural advantage over the Egyptians and God saw to it that the Egyptians would not catch up. As you run with the vision ask God for some supernatural advantage to attain it. (Jeremiah 29: 11) says:

> "For I know the plans I have for you", declares the Lord, "plans to prosper you and not to harm you, plans to give you hope and a future…"

In the parable of the talents, (Matthew 25: 1-30), the one who had been given one talent lacked vision. Instead he hid the talent he was given. When the three servants were given the talents according to their abilities, they were given options as to what they could do with them. The master cried out to the one who had hid his talent that at least he could have deposited the money with the bankers. You have options to set out your vision, no one will do it for you. The one who had been given one talent had a bad attitude towards his master and his talents. This bad attitude caused him not to be visionary.

A vision is something that can become. This is the point that the one with one talent missed, what could become of his one talent. Had he been visionary, that one talent could have become two talents, four talents or more. A vision helps us to focus and discipline ourselves. Never despise your 'small' talent. Never despise the days of small beginnings because a vision starts from where you are.

Do not compare your vision with someone else's. The servant who was given one talent probably compared it with the one who had been given two talents and five talents. This can be very discouraging. Never compare visions. The servants were given talents according to their abilities. We are all unique as individuals and businesses. We might be operating in the same market but have totally different visions. Respect your vision and acknowledge other people's vision. If you are into comparing visions you might end up living other people's lives and not the life purposed for you by God.

There is no vision that is too big. Ask God to give you provision for your vision.

The servant who hid his one talent became cursed instead of blessed. He was labelled 'wicked and lazy.' This servant was cursed because he had no vision. A vision acted upon is supposed to bring some rewards. A vision not acted upon or no vision at all attracts curses. The man with one talent was not productive at all in the absence of his master.

Great men and women in history are great because they saw what other people were not seeing. It is their tenacity that helped them achieve their visions.

Walt Disney's vision statement is "To make people happy." They see happy and smiling faces in advance. What do you see in advance? I hope you see success in advance. A story is told of a function that Walt Disney's wife attended to celebrate the achievements and success of Walt Disney, even though he had passed away.

The celebrations were so magnificent that one person whispered into her ears that if only Walt Disney were alive he would have been proud of the firm's success. The wife replied that he had already seen it many years ago, and that that was why all those people were celebrating that day. This is the power of vision at work. Walt Disney experienced that success and moment many years before it happened. He was a true visionary. You should be able to see and experience your business succeeding even before it has happened. Even when things seem to be going on in the opposite direction, hold on to your vision. Remember not everyone is seeing what you are seeing. Architects are such people. They can be inspirational.

No one could have imagined the potential that was there in making cartoons. Cartoons have been used because many of us would rather be involved in technical, sophisticated white collar businesses. Walter Elias Disney had a vision of making it big in the cartoon industry. For most of us in Africa if you tell your parents and friends that you want to be a cartoonist or that you see potential in the cartoon industry, they will probably laugh at you. Your gift is not someone else's gift.

Cartoons are potentially a laughable matter to venture into, but despite this, someone had a vision in this industry. So is selling vegetables, fish, tomatoes and onions at the market place but if you have a vision you can make a huge success and fortune out of these potentially laughable businesses.

When reflecting back on his success, Walt was quoted as saying: "I hope we'll never lose sight of one thing – that it was all started by a mouse."

Walt went to high school and ended up drawing cartoons. During high school he enrolled in special classes at the Chicago Academy of Fine Arts. At the age of 19 Walt told his parents about his future, in other words his vision. His father did not support his idea.

Despite this he worked hard to realize his vision by first creating "Alice in cartoonland", "Oswald the rabbit" and the popular "Mickey Mouse." Despite having declared bankruptcy in one of his companies, the 'Laugh-O-Gram Company', he held on to his dream tenaciously. Never let any vicissitudes of life fade your vision. A blurred vision is as good as not having one at all. A blurred vision will produce blurred results. Blurred results will keep you in the pool of mediocrity forever.

Walt saw a lack of quality in the existing amusement parks and started having some ideas. He began to match the opportunity with his vision. Later on Disneyland was conceived. In 1954 work started in Los Angeles on building Disneyland. His vision was so big that he wanted to build bigger facilities to end the long queues. He started buying land in Florida to house his vision. He was acting on his vision. He made conscious moves to realize his dreams. At the same time he did not delegate his vision. He could have delegated his dreams to his brother Roy. Walt decided to act on them much to the amusement of Roy. He ran with his vision.

33 000 people showed up on the opening day of the park. There are people out there who will come to witness the realization of your vision. Support at the conception of your vision may be low but once you run with the vision and succeed people will surely come and witness the success. Never give up on your vision, visions that make the world a better place.

Walt Disney had an admirable staying power. He kept at it despite the challenges he faced. One of the challenges he had was doing something that nobody had done before. He faced challenges during the days of "Oswald the rabbit" but he kept at it, he stayed on. It is one thing to start something and it is another to keep at it. This involves closing your mind to negative and discouraging influences. All successful entrepreneurs have developed their staying power. Businesses that are founded on whims never last. You can't develop a staying power on a whim-based foundation.

Not all fires last, it depends on the material used. Some entrepreneurs start with fire and zeal but unfortunately the material used might be that of maize cobs. It can look like a fire from afar but you will be disappointed when you get closer. Statistics show very disappointing failure rate of start ups in the first two years. Ensure you have the right material to keep the fire burning. The strong materials are the ones described in this book. It is imperative that you develop your staying power. When faced with negative thoughts during tough times just say to yourself, 'I am here to stay.' Repeat it as many times as possible. Speak to the situation.

Funding a good vision can be very expensive. When Roy told Walt that there was no fund to support his projects or vision, he replied "…as long as there is imagination left in the world, Disneyland will continue to grow." Where there is a vision there is a way. You have to look for options of funding the vision. Good visions that are life changing don't come cheap.

Just see the work that Dr. David Oyedepo in Nigeria has done. Their church had to do some investments in order to fulfil their vision. These included a 50 000 capacity sanctuary, the Faith Tabernacle, over 250 buses commuting worshippers to and fro church, a plane for missions. Dr Oyedepo also pioneered the establishment of Covenant University. This is investing in a vision at work.

Your vision to have a successful business will not come cheap even at that level where you are. We have some innate abilities in us, use your creative abilities to ensure there is funding for your vision. Many people in this world, especially our part of the world, like to have things for free. Even blessings are not for free. When Isaac wanted to bless Esau he asked him go hunting for some wild game and prepare him some tasty food first. He had to eat first before releasing the blessing to Esau.

When you show tenacity surely God will make a provision for your vision. First you have to use that power or talent He gave you.

Share your vision with your wife or husband. Your spouse is the one who will have a direct impact on your zeal to fulfil your vision. We mostly exclude our spouses in our business ventures. This is a big mistake. Once our spouses buy our vision they can offer encouragement and continuity.

In 1928, Walt wanted to name the famous mouse, 'Mortimer Mouse', but Lilian his wife told him that Mortimer sounded too formal. She suggested the name 'Mickey'. The name 'Mickey Mouse' became a success. This successful name came from Walt's spouse. A spouse can ensure continuity to your dreams. Walt died in 1966 and Lillian carried the torch of trying to fulfil her husband's dream. Lillian died in 1997 but for 31 years after the death of her husband, she worked hard to bring his dream to fruition.

After establishing your vision or dream, ensure you match opportunities with the dream. Grab the opportunities as they come. The men of God should pray for your business. At the time you are starting, during the years of success and during turbulent periods. The familiarity spirit should not control you. Just because we are used to arity spirit should not control you. Just because we are used to seeing our pastors and priests on a daily or weekly basis we might end up missing the opportunity of them speaking life into the business. Let them pray over your vision so that it comes to pass. Do not be like the men of Jericho who had problems with their water and unproductive land. Elijah had visited them but they never put forth their problems to him.

Only when they realized that Elijah had ascended into heaven and later Elisha split the river Jordan into two for them to pass did they see that they could miss an opportunity of having their problems resolved. They confessed amongst themselves that the spirit of Elijah was resting on Elisha. Nevertheless Elisha had succeeded Elijah and they seized the opportunity right away to present their problems of the bad water and barren land. Elisha performed a miracle and the Lord healed the water and barren land. Never take for granted the role of the men of God in your business. Allow them to pray for your vision.

Nelson Rolihlahla Mandela had a vision of a democratic and free society, South Africa, in which all persons lived together in harmony and with equal opportunities. He held this vision tenaciously. He held strongly the belief that South Africa was the richest country in Africa and it could be one of the richest countries in the world as well. What surprised him were the extremes that existed at that time. This did not destroy his vision or ideals. He was in prison from August 1962 to 11 February 1990, yet held on to his vision.

The life of Mandela is inspirational. He was in prison and held on to his vision. He was given an opportunity, in the 1980s, to be released with conditions which would have compromised his vision but he refused. He stated that only free men can negotiate. Most of us are free men and women and yet we allow our vision to fade. Here is a man who was given opportunities to compromise but refused. What is one year of failure in life or business? Here is a man who spent 28 years behind bars protecting his vision, the vision of a democratic and free society, with racial harmony. He refused to accept a permanent state of inferiority. All entrepreneurs should learn from the ideals and tenacity of Nelson Mandela.

Step out of your comfort zone and pursue your vision. Staying at the same place and level will not help you at all. You have to move out from your familiar and safe environment in pursuit of excellence.

Just do it, take some action. Peter, a disciple of Jesus, is the only human being who can describe how it feels like to walk on water. He stepped out of the boat. We know that later on Peter became a great and powerful head of the apostles. In other words he became a great leader, (Matthew 14: 24-32). Do not limit yourself, breakdown the limit walls as you run with your vision.

Step out and learn new useful skills. These new skills will help you attain your vision. Spend your time doing and not talking. When you take action something is bound to happen. Learn to be a 'go-getter'. Don't allow yourself to swim in the pool of familiarity and mediocrity.

For God to support your vision you should also play your part. God is Yahweh-Yireh, "the Lord will provide." He will make a provision for your vision if you also play your part. You have to grow to the level of your vision. It is of no use stagnating and not growing knowledge-wise and spiritually. Read more books, invest in financial literature and spiritual literature. Read the word of God. Pray deep prayers. Start blessing others. Start tithing. Start being a blessing to others. Start being involved in the ministries of your church. There is a tendency for believing that someone else will do the works of mercy. In other words increase your capacity to be blessed. Make room for the blessings. Make room for what God is about to do in your life and business. Make room for things to happen. Do not stagnate. Do something worthwhile. (Isaiah 54: 2) says:

> Enlarge the place of your tent, and let them stretch out the curtains of your dwellings; do not spare, lengthen your cords, and strengthen your stakes.

Your part in the vision is to:

- enlarge the place of your tent
- stretch out the curtains
- lengthen your cords
- strengthen your stakes

This clearly shows that you have a role to play, a pivotal role. Increase your capacity to fulfil the vision. Most of the times we want God to do everything. If you remain where you are and be lukewarm, the vision will end up being just a mere figment of your imagination.

Reverend Doctor Kwabena Darko of Ghana is a successful businessman in Ghana. He started his poultry company Darko Farms & Company four decades ago [40 years ago]. They now supply over 50% of Ghana's poultry requirements. He states that 'God gave me a vision to support His servants with what I had – a poultry farm.' This sounds rather strange in the eyes of men. God has guided him over the years so that he fulfils this vision. Dr Darko states that "I'm not a self-made man, I'm a God-made man." He decided to put God first in his business and let Him lead the way of making a provision for the vision.

Chapter 2

TRAINING FOR SUCCESS

Training is not only achieved in class whereby you get lectures and sit for exams. There is also training through experience. Sometimes when going through the training process you might not necessarily be aware that you are being trained for great things in future.

Never grumble or complain too much when going through some hardships, it is part of the training. For a business to be strong and resilient, the leaders should have gone through some intensive training, not only theoretical but practical, hands-on, painful training as well.

Training establishes a good foundation for your business. If you want to build a sky scrapper you have to dig a very deep foundation. If you are building a small or average house, the foundation needs not be as deep as that of a big 5-storey building. A shallow foundation can't support a high building. Your business needs a good foundation. It is not only academic training but also hands-on painful training. How big do you want your business to be? If very big, then be prepared to have a deep and strong foundation.

The training of Moses, David, Joseph, Elisha and Daniel was by divine intervention. These are men who were made in the same image as God just like you and me. They went through a process of training, the process was not easy, it was by no means a stroll in the park. What we must understand is that it is the process that makes you tenacious and successful. It is the process that ushers you into your destination. You have to be ready. A war is won the day before the actual battle. This means your training was very thorough. The seat-and-wait approach does not apply if you are to reach the land of milk and honey.

These great men applied the theory and experience they had received. Many of us when we receive our certificates, diplomas and degrees we expect the attained qualifications to work for us.

A certificate, diploma or degree is a confirmation that you are capable of reaching great heights in the area studied but it is not a guarantee that you will be successful. It simply confirms your potential. What will determine your success is the process, the application of the things learnt. The process refers to the conscious move of actualizing your dreams. Application with a positive mindset, remember you always bump into what you say and think. Think good things, you will bump into good things. Say good things, you will bump into good thinks and act accordingly. The reverse is true as well.

Joseph's Training

Joseph could interpret dreams. That was his dominant gift or major gift. He was a good leader and organizer that was his minor gift. We should all utilize our God given dominant, major or first gift. After developing your major gift also take time to develop your minor gift.

A dominant or major gift makes way for you. It makes room for you. A minor gift establishes you. When you are employed or working take time to develop both your major and minor gifts. Along the way as you become an entrepreneur, your business can be based on either of the two gifts. It is not always the major gift that you venture into as an entrepreneur but it makes way. It is well and good if you venture into something that brings out your major gift.

A professional golfer's dominant gift is playing golf. His or her minor gift can be developing a brand name such as having his or her name printed on T-shirts, caps, shorts or appearing in commercials. You can be extremely good with calculations and be an accountant, that is a dominant gift. A minor gift can be writing books.

Write down on a piece of paper what you think is your major gift and minor gift. This cannot be done overnight, take your time. Begin to plan how you can use your major gift because it is the one that makes room for the minor gift to come out.

As mentioned, Joseph's dominant or major gift was interpreting dreams and his minor gift was an organizer or leader. The experiences he went through enabled him to develop both gifts, the dominant and minor gift.

Joseph interpreted dreams and experienced the following at each stage,

His own dream	→ Butler and Baker's dream	→ Pharaoh's dream
Accused	→ Forgotten	→ Made Governor
Pit	→ Prison	→ Prominence

Joseph's road to being Governor of Egypt started in a pit. He did not accidentally fall into this pit, he was cast into the pit by his own brothers. As entrepreneurs we are sometimes discouraged when we start from the bottom. We are discouraged when we start with no capital. It is not the capital that matters but your dream. You will find that you have a dream to start a business and it is always people close to you that usually disappoint you, do not be discouraged, it is part of the training process.

We all go through different experiences and trials because our level of greatness and success will differ. If you have a big dream be prepared to go through some tough training and do not be discouraged during the process. This can include walking long distances to your shop or workplace; it is part of the training. Do not look at the big cars that pass you by, just hold on to your dream. Joseph's greatness started in the pit.

Reuben, one of Joseph's brothers, tried to rescue Joseph. His other brothers had suggested on killing Joseph. Reuben is the one who suggested on throwing him into the pit rather than kill him. As you start your business God will place some people in your life to hold your hand. You have to be willing to be helped. Help is not only in someone giving you start up capital but it comes in various forms in a way that your dream is not killed. If Joseph had been killed, the plans God had for him would have been killed as well. The reason why you still breathe today is because God has already placed some people in your life to keep your dream alive. If you think you are alone, think twice or rather look twice. Capital is not the only answer. (Romans 8: 28) says:

> And we know that all things work together for good to those who love God, to those who are called according to His purpose.

God has a purpose for all of us. The proof is the proof of life. It is said that the grave is a very rich place because a lot of people are buried with their potential. The sum total of the unused potential is rich. Use that potential in line with the gift of life that you have now.

Joseph's brothers were actually contributing to his next level of training, the market place. The Ishmaelites started trading Joseph in the market place. He learnt how business was traded in the market place, he saw people come in and go out of the market. Joseph learnt how people negotiated and did business at the market place. Eventually Joseph was sold to Potiphar, who was an officer at Pharaoh's palace. Joseph graduated from the market place to Potiphar's luxurious house.

That was the next level of training as an overseer in Potiphar's house. He was given authority in the house. Joseph learnt how to delegate, command and inspect. His training in human resources had just begun. He had to learn people skills. To be second in command to Pharaoh was not an easy task. That meant managing all the people in Egypt. This all started by managing people in a household set up. In other words Joseph had to crawl, take baby steps before he could leap. Most of us want to leap before we can crawl. Start small and think big.

How you relate to your two employees will determine how you relate to a hundred employees when your business grows. It is possible to start developing good people skills with just two employees. If you can influence two people to do what you expect to be done then adding more people will not be a major problem for you. Potiphar was a man of influence and Joseph had to learn how to lead an influential life.

There is an old saying that "charity begins at home but does not end there." You should be challenged that "people skills start with one person and will not end there." It is dangerous to despise the days of small beginnings. Sharpen your personal communication skills, learn the art of persuasion whilst still small. Have you have ever seen how some 'big fish' are poor at communicating? It is often because they started big or never sharpened their people skills when they were small. There is no one born with poor communication skills. It is a learned behaviour.

When you start well accusations and persecution seem to persist. Joseph later graduated and went to prison. Potiphar's wife had to lie in order to send Joseph to his next level of training – that is, being in charge of bad guys in prison. Joseph had to learn how to extend the art of persuasion to the bad guys so that even they could obey him. This is some tough training. Just when you thought you had become prosperous, you wind up in prison. This is a bitter pill to swallow but it is part of the training.

The prison warden put Joseph in charge of all those held in prison. Just imagine a prisoner giving out instructions to other fellow prisoners. This is where he had to really practice the art of persuasion otherwise he would have really got them extremely angry.

Joseph began to exercise his minor gift of leadership and persuasion. Prison also presented him with an opportunity to exercise his dominant or major gift of interpreting dreams. You can use both your major and minor gifts wherever you are. Here is someone who used both gifts in prison. Therefore as entrepreneurs we should stop grumbling and complaining how tough our environment is, be it economic or political environment.

Joseph interpreted the dreams of the butler and the baker, making use of his dominant gift. It is unfortunate that the butler forgot about Joseph when he was released. He only remembered Joseph two years later when Pharaoh needed someone to interpret his dreams. The magicians and wise men of Egypt failed to interpret Pharaoh's dream. This required Joseph to use his major gift. After interpreting Pharaoh's dream it earned Joseph the position of Governor of Egypt. Pharaoh gave Joseph power over the Egyptians,

(Genesis 41: 44)

"...and without your consent no man may lift his hand or foot in all the land of Egypt."

Even Potiphar was not allowed to lift his hand or foot without Joseph's consent. Pharaoh did not even ask why Joseph had been imprisoned. He just called for Joseph to interpret his dream – to exercise his dominant gift. These good days are coming where people will not ask you where you have been but just want you to exercise your major and minor gifts. Joseph overtook Potiphar in authority, he was flowing in the over-takers anointing.

It was not clear at first with all the hurdles that Joseph was facing that they were preparing him for this top post in Egypt. He came to Egypt as a prisoner and later occupied the number two position in Egypt. He now had to use the people skills he had learnt. He now had to use the leadership skills he had learnt throughout the turbulent years. He now used his ability to organize things to store 20% of the harvest for the lean years. He had to use the art of persuasion to both the good and bad people in Egypt in order to prepare them for the seven years of drought. The drought was going to affect the good and the bad, the rich and the poor. He had to control trading at the market places, where he was once traded. Joseph now knew the dynamics of the markets, the trading places. He learnt these dynamics when the Ishmaelites were trying to sell him at the market place.

Take the hardships you face as learning points. Do not be quick to speak out, put God first and you will find favour in His sight. Nobody said it would be easy or a walk in the park when delving into the world of entrepreneurship.

David's Training

Shepherd → Musician → Leader of society's outcasts → King

David's road to being King of Israel started from keeping or tending sheep. Animal husbandry is a branch of agriculture. David's dominant gift was that of shepherding.

While herding sheep David gained some leadership skills. When one sheep went astray it meant looking for it until it joined the herd. When one sheep goes missing out of a flock of hundred, it means looking for it until it is found. This taught David to look out for people placed under him. In (1 Samuel 23), David enquired of the Lord to save the people of Keliah from the hands of the Philistines. David and his men saved the people of Keliah.

A true leader fights for those he leads. A true leader defends those he leads. A true leader corrects the lost with compassion. David learnt all these qualities while he was a shepherd boy. David later had compassion over Mephibosheth, Jonathan's disabled son. He started where he was with what he had – a shepherd's staff, rod and the sheep in his charge. Some of us want to start big and demand a bigger platform to exercise our abilities. Life can be very disappointing if this mindset persists.

The shepherd's staff had a cradle, the S shape at the tip of it. This was meant to pull out any sheep that had fallen into a crevice by first hooking it and pulling it out gently. David used the tools he had at hand to carry out duties that later became significant in his life. Never despise the days of small beginnings – use the available tools at hand to nurture your talent.

David, one of the main authors of the Psalms, also developed his minor gift using examples of the staff and rod – the tools he had as a shepherd. The skills you learn now can be used to develop your minor gift. The Spirit inspired – prayers and praises of (Psalm 23: 4) says:

> Even though I walk through the valley of the shadow of death, I will fear no evil, for you are with me; your rod and your staff, they comfort me.

When you reach the next level of glory, do not forget the skills you learnt from the previous level of glory. Do not be embarrassed about them. Just imagine a king talking about a staff and rod. One would think he would only be talking about swords.

The shepherd's STAFF can be used to represent:

S – See
T – Talent
A – Action
F – Faith
F – Father

Look around you and learn to **see** opportunities. There are moments of opportunities that can change your life both in service and business. Use your God-given **talent** to make use of those opportunities. Take **action** and do not procrastinate. Have **faith** and know that the **Father** in heaven is watching over you. Remember we do not move by sight alone but with faith. Faith sustains your staying power.

When you are a shepherd, even if you have a hundred sheep under your care, you end up knowing each and every one of your sheep. This enabled David to learn to remember names when he became king of Israel. Some entrepreneurs with 20 employees may not easily remember their names. It is very important to remember the names of your employees from the manager to the messenger. It brings joy to the support staff that even the owner knows his or her name. That joy is surprisingly linked to productivity.

During David's humble beginnings he fought a bear and a lion. Those were the challenges that he faced at the level he was. He did not take it lightly. When David was about to fight Goliath he explained to Saul how he had rescued his sheep from the mouth of a bear and lion. David started explaining to Saul the art of war, striking it and seizing it by the hair. This must have astonished Saul, that David could compare such an encounter with the battle before hand of fighting Goliath, the giant. David went through what he went through so that he could be a point of reference. David's point of reference was a lion and a bear. When he explained to Saul his encounters with the bear and lion, David never downplayed the role of God in all this. He acknowledged how God had delivered him from the paw of the lion and the bear. When giving a testimony of your success as an entrepreneur never down-play the hand of God in it, mention it when you testify.

Never look down upon your CV if there are some diplomas and degrees missing on it. You carry something that at an appointed time will manifest itself. If the diplomas and degrees are missing, it is never too late to start making the first steps to acquire them. David's point of reference was the challenges he faced at the level he was. You can be fresh from school or college and want to delve into the world of entrepreneurship, your points of reference are the achievements and challenges you faced at school. Remember S.T.A.F.F.

David's minor gift of a musician – playing the harp ensured that he came into contact with King Saul. In fact he became one of King Saul's armour-bearers through music. David would play the harp for Saul and the spirit upon Saul would depart and he would feel better. While in King Saul's service David also learnt how a king lives. He learnt how a king gives orders to his subjects. He was going through some training through music. We all have different talents, a musician can also be a powerful entrepreneur. Use any talent you have to establish yourself for success in the future. By the time David became king, he had already learnt how a king lives therefore did not act strangely when ascended to the throne.

You can be a junior in an audit firm, law firm or consulting firm, never look down upon yourself. Try to learn how the partners go about with their business. Be patient because one day you may become a partner. Many people waste time complaining that their salaries are low. Don't join that train because you are getting training that goes beyond your current salary. Remember S.T.A.F.F. Learn from David; he was already anointed by Samuel as future king of Israel by the time he was playing the harp for King Saul. David did not rush to King Saul and tell him that he was anointed as king of Israel already. This was delayed gratification at work. David was calm, cool and collected. Patience is a virtue.

The day of revelation and the day of manifestation are different.

Even his father mistook David for an ordinary boy. Jesse did not fully understand what his son was carrying. He was stopped from going to battle and his father sent him on an errand to just provide food to his brothers in battle and come back home. When starting out as an entrepreneur not even your parents or people close to you may fully understand what drives you. Never be discouraged. The good thing that David did was that he still obeyed his father. He never boasted that he was the future king of Israel – not even to his relatives. Don't savour ties with your folks because you are going to be a successful entrepreneur or that you are now successful. David demonstrated delayed gratification. He never complained that his father was sending the future king of Israel on small errands such as delivering food. When most of us make our first million, we become "untouchable".

A lot of entrepreneurs expect immediate results after injecting some seed capital into the business. The initial days can be turbulent, you can start with losses for a number of months or years before breaking-even and moving into profitability. Be patient. Yes you have a vision, take your time to fulfil it, run with patience.

Patience will not only be required in the area of profitability but also in other areas such as human resources, customer relations, supplier relations, relations with the bank. It takes time before your employees will come to fully trust you, it takes time for customers to believe in your products and services, it takes time for suppliers to trust you that they will get consistent payments, it takes time for the bank to give you the much needed loan. Come up with six to ten ways of raising funds without knocking at the door of the bank.

Be patient. God will give you double if you trust in him. Don't be discouraged if you only have a handful or customers or clients. In His time he will multiply them. (Isaiah 61: 7) says:

> Instead of their shame my people will receive a double portion, and instead of disgrace they will rejoice in their inheritance; and so they will inherit a double portion in their land, and everlasting joy will be theirs.

For every season there is a purpose and for every purpose there is a time. We might be in the same season but in different times.

On his way to kingship David became leader of society's outcasts in Adullam. They were about four hundred men. Just like Joseph who was made leader of the prisoners whilst he was a prisoner himself, David had to go through a similar type of training. Never look down on people. The people at the bottom are the ones who will push you up and the ones at the top will pull you up.

David fought successful battles with these men up to the time he was established as king of Israel. David used the art of persuasion to become the leader of these dejected people who were in debt and distress. His leadership style convinced them that he should be their leader. He trained these men who were later known as 'David's mighty men'. He took them from their low self esteem to become men of substance. It is one thing to be a boss and another to be a leader. David's leadership skills and God's favour catapulted him to the throne.

David had a high EQ, emotional intelligence quotient. When the army of Israel was being insulted by Goliath, David asked the men standing near him what would be given to the man that would kill Goliath. When Eliab, David's oldest brother heard him speaking to the men, he became furious and shouted at David. David held his peace and asked Eliab why he was refusing him the right to speak. He turned away and continued asking other men the same question. David could have replied his brother with anger or retaliate, remember David had fought a bear and a lion before. David kept his cool and exercised a high degree of emotional intelligence. He didn't want to cause a scene.

King Saul tried to kill David several times. When David had the opportunity to kill Saul he restrained from doing it. In this case he took control of his emotions. It was an emotional situation that David for one had been anointed as future king of Israel, that David had calmed the spirits that tormented the man trying to kill him, that David had defeated Goliath the Philistine who was insulting the army of Israel, that David was Saul's son in law. Despite all this David refrained from killing Saul. David kept his emotions under control.

After the Amalekites had raided Ziklag, they took into captive the wives, sons and daughters of David and his men. The six hundred men pursued the Amalekites. Only four hundred men managed to continue with the pursuit. The other two hundred were too tired to continue. David did not put these men to the sword or accuse them but continued with the pursuit. The four hundred managed to destroy the Amalekites and rescue their families. In addition they came back with some plunder.

On return David met the two hundred men who had given up. David greeted them. He held back his emotions even though these two hundred men had given up while his family was being held hostage by the Amalekites. Some of us could have burst out with anger towards these men just like some among the men of David that had continued with the pursuit. They refused to share the plunder with them but David commanded that they should all share the plunder with the two hundred men that gave up the chase. Such control of emotions is very rare.

Many of us entrepreneurs need to learn how to control our emotions. At the touch of a button we freak out. We yell from left, right and centre. You only make the situation worse. We end up having employees who have resigned constructively. They are there but have no commitment towards their work. To be a successful entrepreneur you have to have a high EQ.

This was the training process for David. He used both his major and minor gifts to reach greatness. He used what he had and his experience as a shepherd boy. David enquired of the Lord many times.

All this was part of the training, of preparing him for greatness. When greatness came he was adequately prepared. Whatever God is doing in your life it will be manifested one day.

Daniel's Experience

There are two lessons to be drawn from Daniel's experiences. Firstly we must be different in our approach to things and secondly we learn that one can do well in a foreign land.

Daniel acted differently from the others. When the young men were brought to Babylon they were given royal food and wine. Daniel resolved that he would not defile himself by eating the king's delicacies. He was very young then, around sixteen years old. Daniel challenged that he would look better in ten days after eating vegetables and drinking water. After the guard's inspection this proved to be true, Daniel and the other three looked healthier and better nourished than the other men.

Most often entrepreneurs run into the temptation of mob psychology – that is following what the group is up to. He and the other three chose to be different. Once you are different that will be an automatic competitive advantage over others. It might seem strange to be different, other people may even regard you as being crazy. You will be surprised that once you do things differently for good, others will follow. Ten days of trial had an impact for three years. After ten days when Daniel and his friends looked healthier the diet for the whole group was changed for the whole three years whiles undergoing training. Think differently, don't just follow the crowd. Come up with unique marketing plans and strategies because if you do the same thing that others are doing, the customer or client will not be able to differentiate your offerings from what others are offering.

The same spirit of acting differently landed Daniel in trouble when prayers were offered for thirty days under King Darius. He continued praying. When you act different you, may irritate others. Being different comes with its own costs. Daniel was thrown into a den of lions for being different and exceptional. Just before Daniel was promoted, the administrators and satraps in Babylon plotted against him. It is said that in war you can easily identify your enemy but in business it is difficult because anybody can be your enemy. The enemy is not so visible.

God always comes to the rescue in such matters. It is not everyone who will be happy with your success as a result of being different.

Daniel was prosperous in the foreign land of Babylon. He was made third in command by King Belshazzar. If you are an entrepreneur who has set up a business in a foreign country, there is a likelihood that you will excel. Discipline and desisting from cultural myopia will be the key. There are conditions to this, (Isaiah 1: 19) says:

> If you are willing and obedient, you shall eat the good of the land.

Daniel was obedient to God and he exercised his dominant gift of interpreting dreams, which led him to being prosperous in a foreign land.

Moses' Experience

There arose a king over Egypt who did not know Joseph. This was approximately 220 years after Joseph's death. He disliked the success and progress of the Israelites. It is tough to imagine that the good that Joseph had done had been forgotten. There are people whom we bring along into our enterprises that will not necessarily appreciate your humble beginnings. Be patient with them. Ensure you preserve the history of your enterprise, take photographs. These will be important in the future.

Moses was the right man for the job to lead the people of Israel out of Egypt. He was an Israelite who grew up in the knowledge and wisdom of Egyptians. All that time he was being trained for that purpose. Moses never forgot his identity even though he was living a life of luxury in Pharaoh's house.

Moses fled from Egypt to Midian and stayed there for forty years. This was his first desert experience. He later experienced a similar desert experience, in the same region – the Desert of Sinai, when leading the Israelites to the Promised Land. Moses was 80 years old when God first made contact with him. It is never too late for God to make contact with you and your enterprise.

Moses had his own doubts whether Pharaoh would listen to him. Then God asked Moses what was in his hand. Moses replied that he had a rod. He cast it onto the ground as per God's instructions and it turned into a serpent. This was one of the miraculous signs Moses was to perform in Egypt. The key lesson here is that God used what Moses had in his hands and not what he had left at home. God can use what you have and where you are to do great things. Never look down upon what you have; you might see it as small or useless but God will turn it into something big. Look at both hands and say 'God can use these hands.'

Moses carelessly took the law into his own hands by killing an Egyptian. His anger overpowered him. This was not the right time to act. The day of revelation is different from the day of manifestation. Failure to realize this made him a fugitive. He failed to realize that the battle was not his but the Lord's. Later Moses became an ambassador of God. He now did things God's way 40 years later.

In the natural realm it was not possible that the children of Israel would cross the Red Sea. The Lord parted the Red Sea. All these signs, including the 10 plagues, increased Moses' faith and confidence in God. Despite the negativity and pessimism that surrounded him he assured the children of Israel that God would see them through. In the wilderness, the children of Israel always complained about not having enough food and water.

Moses interceded on behalf of the Israelites. He showed the power of intercessory prayer. When Moses was up on Mount Sinai for 40 days and 40 nights, the Israelites were busy making a false idol in the form of a golden calf. God saw this and instantly wanted to destroy the Israelites but Moses intervened and pleaded with God not to destroy them, (Exodus 32: 11-14). God changed His mind because of Moses' plea. Intercessory prayers are very important for our businesses.

Disobeying God's direct orders comes at a cost. Moses learnt this the hard way. As the leader and someone who had direct access to God, he should have known this. God asked Moses to speak out to the rock and God would cause water to come out. Instead of speaking to the rock, Moses lifted his hand and struck the rock twice with his rod, (Numbers 20: 7-13). The level of spirituality that Moses was operating, and where God was using him as a vessel required him to be in perfect obedience to God. When operating at this level, it is perilous to do things your own way.

Elisha's Training

The account of Elijah and Elisha teaches us the power of mentorship. Elisha later took over from Elijah as a great prophet. Elisha requested with persistence a double portion of Elijah's spirit. Elisha's request was granted and he later performed great miracles starting with parting the River Jordan.

Find a mentor who will teach you the ropes in business. Don't underestimate your mentor. Elijah had a servant when he fled from Jezebel. The servant stayed in Beersheba in Judah while Elijah kept on running, this time heading for the desert. This servant remained behind and left his master running because he looked down on Elijah. How could he follow someone who was running away from a woman? What the servant failed to realize was that Elijah was a man of God despite his fleeing.

I have a mentor who tells me that he only looks at the top line and bottom line. He argues that the finer details in the middle is handled by the people he employs.

Chapter 3

THE POWER OF POSITIVE THINKING

Let the weak say they are strong, let the blind say they can see, let the poor say they are rich. Left brainers would probably dismiss this, as everything has to be logical and factual. I would have probably dismissed the above statements if I had not discovered the right and the sub-conscious brain. I have a strong left brain and now paying attention to my right brain and sub conscious. You never know I may start singing soon.

Everybody goes through a process of internal dialogue. You are always talking to yourself. The question is, "what do you tell yourself about yourself?" Defeating messages or messages of victory? As I talk to myself, I do my best to fill my mind with positive thoughts. As an entrepreneur, always attempt to be a positive thinker, this is a valuable asset. You are going to face tough times and what you tell yourself will determine your success or failure. It is not what people tell you that counts but what you tell yourself during the times of internal dialogue.

Always dream in colour and not in black and white. Attempt to ACTUALIZE YOUR DREAMS. You should remember that dreaming is free. Big things start with a dream, a big dream and not planning. After dreaming then ideas are generated and later screened and so forth. Never play down the power of dreams in our lives. People should not define the level, which you should dream. They should not tell you to be realistic and dream within reason. The mere fact that you are staying in the ghetto does mean you can't dream big. The mere fact that you live in a grass-thatched house does not give other people the right to limit your dreams. Find a passion and hold on to your dream. A lot of people's positive ideas are thrashed by others, mainly by opinion leaders. Never let opinion leaders take away your dreams.

Visualize how your business will look like in five years. You will be amazed at the effect this will have on you despite whatever set backs you may be currently experiencing.

A long time ago my brother made a powerful revelation to me. He told me that God did well to create us with a silent mind. I mean not knowing what the other person is thinking. If we knew or could hear what the other person is thinking, there would be chaos in the world – never ending wars, family feuds, divorces – the list will be endless. So think positively, that will make the world a better place.

There can be many theories advanced when it comes to positive thinking but the most important is the process of internal dialogue. What do you tell yourself about yourself? At least that is the starting point of how people will see and treat you. This applies to both employees and employers. Have you ever seen leaders who have no self-confidence or seem confused? I have seen plenty of them, you will be surprised what they tell themselves. Great leaders who ooze charisma have mastered the art of positive thinking through a healthy internal dialogue. This is a must for professional salesmen and saleswomen.

One morning I woke up and told t myself that I was going to exercise the power of positive thinking. I did not tell my wife as I felt there was no need to announce it. I dropped the children at school, then dropped my wife at work then went to work. From the time I woke up to the time I arrived at work, my efforts were in vain.

After waking up my wife asked me pertinent but mindboggling questions. My children started asking me to buy this and that – despite the fact that I did not have the funds to meet their demands. Just as I arrived at the children's school, the headmaster reminded me about the outstanding school fees. My car's fuel gauge, as I dropped off my wife, was not looking good - so much for positive thinking. Refusing defeat, I started writing down all the negative things that I faced in that one hour. I carefully wrote down each situation in bullet point form and a possible solution. I discovered that 95% of the problems were money-related. At least I pinned down my problems and resolved to expand my means in order to be liquid enough.

Always take stock of your thoughts. Don't be quick to dismiss yourself, some of the problems are not of your making. Let's not be haphazard thinkers. Write down what is bringing you down, and write possible solutions, legal and moral solutions of course. It's human nature for people to listen more to negative thoughts than positive ones. Have you ever noticed how, when you give someone a compliment, maybe his/her hairstyle impressed you, that person quickly dismisses you. Say something negative, you will definitely get his/her attention. It's human nature. To be forewarned is to be forearmed.

Let people call you a daydreamer. At least you dream and look forward to a better tomorrow for yourself and the common good of all. People will say that you live in world of your own. If that world they are talking about is a world of positive thinkers, then stay there. Their world won't get them far.

Dr David Oyedepo observed in his book "In pursuit of Vision" that 'Men only pity those that are in the pit. We are not meant for the pit..." Arise and strengthen your stakes as you run with the vision. When pursuing your vision avoid pity parties. This is a state where you expect everybody to feel pity for you when you fail in something. If a great man like Abraham Lincoln had entertained pity parties he would never have been president of the United States.

Abraham Lincoln failed many times but later became president of the United States of America. The story of Abraham Lincoln is very inspiring. He was a positive thinker. Lincoln lost his job and was defeated for state legislature in 1832, had problems during his days as a postmaster, defeated for nomination for congress, lost renomination, defeated for U.S. senate, defeated for nomination for Vice president, in 1858 was again defeated for U.S. senate. He never gave up. He tried his best to tell us what was going on in his mind. Abraham Lincoln said: 'My great concern is not whether you have failed, but whether you are content with your failure.' He replaced negative thoughts with positive thoughts in order to overcome his setbacks.

After 'failing' he surged on and had his successes. He was elected to the Illinois state legislature, admitted to practice law in the U.S. Supreme Court, elected to congress and finally elected president of the United States in 1860. This is an example of a man who never gave up easily. We should not give up at the first or second hurdle. There is no sweet without sweat. Abraham Lincoln from 1832 to 1860 went through a series of failures and successes until he occupied the highest office in the U.S. Say regularly: 'I know no defeat, whatever problems I am facing today are temporary setbacks.'

Thomas Edison tried more than a thousand times to come up with a light bulb that would work. He kept on trying until he was successful in inventing the light bulb, which we enjoy up to today. Just imagine how frustrating it can be to try about one thousands bulbs and none worked. These great men were positive thinkers who never gave up despite the seemingly hopeless situations they faced.

If you want to build a big and successful business, watch what you tell yourself. Fill your mind with positive thoughts. Replace the negative thoughts with positive ones.

Joshua and Caleb were positive thinkers, (Numbers 13-14). They were amongst the group of people that had been sent by Moses to spy on Canaan. The other men gave a bad report of their mission and complained that there were giants in Canaan and that the spies looked like grasshoppers compared to the giants. Caleb told the congregation or gathering that they should immediately go to Canaan for they would be able to overcome the obstacles. The other ten men saw failure but Joshua and Caleb saw success.

They all saw the same things on their mission in Canaan. The only thing that separated the positive and negative men was what they allowed their minds to believe. The bad report by the ten men caused the whole of Israel to weep for one night. They even thought of going back into bondage in Egypt. They had imparted negative thoughts into so many people. The law of impartation was at work. The same bad report by the ten caused the people to be angry, so angry that they wanted to stone the positive thinkers, Joshua and Caleb. Always remember that not everyone will agree or be happy with your positive thoughts. This is so because the negatives can be so overwhelming. Be prepared for resistance as you radiate positive thoughts.

These are the moments when God shows up. Put God first, like Joshua and Caleb did. They were confident that the Lord was with Israel and He would protect them. God told Moses and Aaron that those who had complained, negative thinkers, would not enter into Canaan. The only people to enter Canaan were those below twenty years old and Joshua and Caleb, the positive thinkers.

Joshua and Caleb did not concentrate on how big the giants in Canaan were, but on how big God is. They replaced negative thoughts with positive thoughts.

You can miss the Promised Land, that flows with milk and honey, because of negative thoughts. Your business can fail to move forward because of the negative thoughts that you fill your mind with. You can increase your market share, you can get new customers, you can obtain funding to finance your start up or expansion plans, just think positively.

Thomas Edison said: "Many of life's failures are people who did not realize how close they were to success when they gave up."

At Walt Disney the power of positive thinking is alive. If your job is to interface with the public or customers, they say you are 'on stage'. If your job does not involve meeting the public, they say you are 'back-stage'. They have stressed to the employees that whether you are 'on stage' or 'back-stage' there is no one better than the other. It is emphasized that those 'on stage' should work together with those 'back-stage' to 'put on the show', a good show for that matter in line with their vision of making people happy.

Many times in our businesses and lives those on stage can really take all the credit and over shadow those that are back-stage. It takes positive thinking to realize that you are working hand-in-hand 'to put on a good show'.

People question that despite thinking positively and reaching a certain level of spirituality, things still go wrong. The most important thing is not to expect instant gratification. You also need to have role models that can help you to surge forward, people who have gone before you. These are people you can learn from.

In his book '*Think Big*' Dr Ben Carson, stated that he did not grow up with his father so he always had some characters in the bible as his role models. People like Daniel and Joseph can be real good role models. Today Dr Ben Carson, is one of the most celebrated paediatric neurosurgeons in the world. He did not achieve this status over night.

Strongholds are more of internal than external events. Strongholds are basically mental in nature. You need to break these strongholds in your mind.

Chapter 4

POSITIVE THINKING – THE GOOD SAMARITAN

How you see things is very important. As mentioned before do you see the glass half full or half empty? You should be like the Good Samaritan. He was able to help the man who fell among thieves and was badly wounded. The priest and the Levite saw the man who had been beaten by the thieves as half dead but the Good Samaritan saw the same man as half alive. The mere fact that the Good Samaritan saw the injured man as half alive prompted him to help him. When we see situations or issues from a positive perspective it prompts us to act positively while the reverse is also true, if we see situations or issues from a negative perspective it prompts us to act negatively. Positive thinking leads to positive actions.

Norman Vincent Peale noted that any fact facing us is not as important as our attitude toward it, for that determines our success or failure. Some facts before us are so terrifying and overwhelming that they can defeat us before we do anything about them. That is where positive attitudes become very useful.

Therefore be warned that a negative attitude repels people and opportunities. SinVyest Tan said, 'don't frown because you never know who is falling in love with your smile.'

The Good Samaritan saved a man's life because he saw him as half alive. He even paid two denarii to the innkeeper for the upkeep of the injured man. He even assured the innkeeper that he would cover the bill, on his return, if it over shot. When you see things from a positive angle, you are ready to invest in what you believe in. The investment is both in the form of time and money. What did the Good Samaritan see in the bed-ridden man? He saw him as half alive, he saw him recovering. In the Good Samaritan's mind was a picture of a man recovering, running up and down.

Always have a mental picture of success. Never let that mental picture fade due to temporary set backs that life presents time and again. You can save lives in this world depending on how you view life in general. You can help to make the world a better place. There is no contribution that is small.

What pictures do you put in your mind when you face adversities or challenging situations? That is what will make you or break you. Never mind about what other people are saying about you, your situation or your business.

Positive thinking can save your business. When your business is going through a rough patch or is in trouble, when hope seems to be a figment of everybody's imagination, do you see the entity as half dead or half alive? This positive thinking, which rises above all problems, including the global financial crisis or great depression, will save your business. When you see the business half alive, it will cause you to come up with workable strategies to revive the business. It releases the creativity hormones in you.

Remember we all have creation in us, we are made in the image of God. God created the heavens and the earth. Therefore you can create your own business and make success out of it, why not?

Unlock that potential. Who taught Adam to name the animals? When God created you, He gave you all the tools to function, to be the best you can be. Our God is a God of resources. You have potential in you. Walt Emerson said 'what lies behind us and what lies before us are tiny matters compared to what lies within us.'

Your success story will be told to future generations. The story of the Good Samaritan is still being told up to today. It all starts with seeing the bottle as half full and not half empty. It all starts with seeing a situation, issues and business as half alive and not half dead. Norman Vincent Peale said 'change your thoughts, and you change your world.' God has already given you the power, all you need to do is to active that God-given ability, which is also referred to as a talent.

In his book *48 Success Habits,* Praise George observed that your positive habits will help you take advantage of financial opportunities that millions of people pass by daily.

Reverend Dr Zacc Kawalala came up with a new word called 'Impossican't'. This is basically a combination of two words, impossible and cannot. He states that we create barriers in our minds most of the time and end up saying that it is impossible and cannot be done. This negative thinking renders us inactive and we end up giving up. When one gives up no action is taken. When no action is taken, we live things to chance.

Chapter 5

WHAT IS MONEY?

There are many books one can read in search of enlightenment on what money is. There has been no greater revelation of what money is, than the one below. This can be life changing so fasten your seat belts.

Money is not that piece of paper that we use to buy things. Rightly put those notes are currencies. Money is an idea. That is true. Shocking as it may sound but money is an idea or ideas. Those pieces of paper or notes are just a confirmation that your idea was good and successful. Why do we have strategy sessions, performance meetings, reviews, board meetings and so on? The reason is to share ideas on how to move forward or better put how to make more money. Once these ideas are sound and put into practice you find the notes flying in. Cash flows in (remember cashflow statements?), profitability improves and net worth increases.

This is so because the ideas worked. You can never make money if your ideas repel money. If your ideas are out of touch with reality, you will never make money. I have interacted with rich people many times and this is true. Just listen to the ideas of rich people, you will be amazed. This is not only in business but also in charity works or works of mercy.

Find an opportunity to chat with rich people. Listen very closely to their ideas. You will see a certain pattern of their thoughts. Listen to a poor man's ideas. You will understand why he or she is poor. These are two polarized economic standings. Their ideas and approach to things are different. Also listen to the middle class people's ideas. It does not take much but to just listen, compare and contrast. Your findings might be shocking. The ideas of these groups are radically different. Some look at things from the bigger picture perspective others from a microcosm viewpoint.

Once you do this, you will concur with me that money really is an idea and the notes and coins are a confirmation that the idea worked. Accountants, economists and financial analysts may be baffled by this revelation. Well it's true that is why some people invest more wisely than others. Making money is all about the idea being successful.

Just follow through the stages of a new product development. Marketers will tell you that it all starts with idea generation, the idea screening and so forth. Ask them, they will tell you. Once the product, service or project is launched successfully then cash flows in. The notes and coins flow in. When you are looking for a better paying job, it starts with an idea to better yourself financially. The unfortunate thing is that situations, people and a host of other factors crush our ideas, some within and some outside our control. When someone crushes your good ideas he or she is denying you an opportunity of making money. Knowing this, you will have an idea of who is, and what is denying you money.

Some people are good at PHDs (pull him down syndromes). They invest a lot of time and effort in trying to pull others down. You have to be careful of such people. They are the worst people who can deny you money. They "go out of their way" to crush your idea. You should develop a sixth sense of quickly identifying these people. Why do think rich people most often keep to themselves?

When you hear someone saying that, "I am broke". It basically means that he or she has run out of ideas. Well one of my pastors says that he is never broke but is in between riches.

There are left brainers, intelligent individuals, dismiss good ideas or revelations. They want to calculate their way through life. Have you ever asked yourself how C students make it? The right brain is associated with artistic and musical abilities.

Being broke or broken is not good or healthy at all. It is as good as running out of ideas, which is not a good thing either. You should once in a while shout aloud "Eureka!" "I have found it!" like Archimedes did. Let's not only clap for others and their glories all the time, its high time other people clapped for us.

Improve your financial literacy if you are going to have good and sound business ideas. A reader is a leader. Invest in financial courses, attend evening lessons after work. In order to come up with good business ideas, you have to differentiate facts and opinions. Money is usually lost when actions are based on opinions. It might look like a good idea but it is based on an opinion and not fact. This applies mostly to investments.

When you invest in financial literacy you will usually be a step ahead in identifying where the money is. Information is in abundance in this 21st century. There is information overload. Don't clutter your mind with unnecessary information, no matter how appealing it may be. To be successful you need to improve your cognitive skills. Sharpening your ability to think and analyze is of paramount importance. There is great need to simplify the complicated and make use of it.

A lot of us like reading general magazines that will not really sharpen our financial intelligence. Financial intelligence leads to more money. Invest in what is relevant and know where to find it. If you cannot do it on your own, leverage with other people's experience and knowledge. Develop symbiotic relationships. You should know and find out who knows what you need to know. There is someone out there in the body of knowledge who has the information you need. Use the internet to your advantage. This is where the ideas come from that lead to paper money.

Chapter 6

SPIRITUAL DIMENSION OF ENTREPRENEURSHIP

When I told my pastor my major challenges in entrepreneurship, he told me that there is a spiritual dimension to business. That revelation has always been in my mind ever since. His recommendation was prayer. There are opposing forces, which work against you when you are trying to get somewhere. These opposing forces come in all shapes and sizes. Some opposing forces do not seem very obvious but are lethal in their effect.

The sad part is that there are so many things that distract us from seeing the spiritual aspects of entrepreneurship. They include unlimited success whilst ignoring the facts aforementioned, pleasure binges, atheism, living a life of utopia. What we must remember is that we are living in a world of awesome progress but paradoxically one of appalling evils. I believe that there are opposing spiritual forces that roam up and about. We do not fight against flesh and blood but against principalities of darkness.

In his book '*7 great principles*' Bishop Dag Heward-Mills states 'the fact that a human being is actually a spirit living inside a physical body is one of the lesser known truths'. 'A human being is not just a piece of meat.' This basically explains that there is a spiritual dimension to our lives.

May our dependence be on God and God alone. Let our help and all our help come from him. May we embrace the spirit of knowledge, the spirit of wisdom and the spirit of the fear of the Lord. Some of our businesses are held back because of generational curses. That is curses that have been passed on from one generation to the other because of sins of our forefathers. These chains of bondage need to be broken. That is why prayer is important; ask God to break those chains of generational curses.

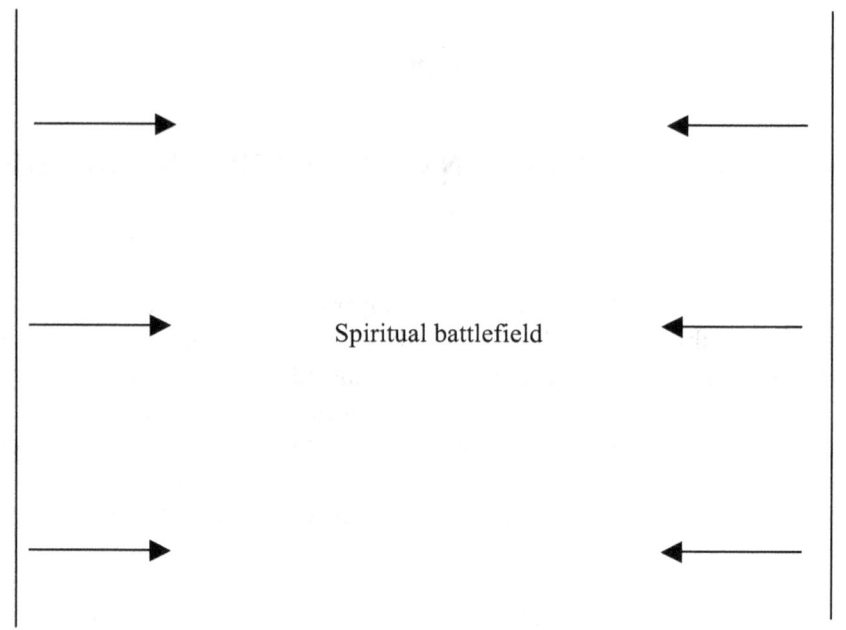

Trying to get somewhere   Opposing Forces

To the land of milk and honey   Trials and tribulations

There are very intelligent but poor people in this world. People with a spectacular dominant left brain, that part of the brain associated with calculations. They can work out complicated formulas in various disciplines but are still financially poor. Sometimes we need to look beyond the physical realm. Unfortunately some people turn to the wrong spirits for guidance. As I mentioned above, may our dependence be on God and God alone.

If you are not sure whether you are in bondage of generational curses, you can just ask God to break them. Yourself as an individual will not know that these chains are keeping you from moving to the next level of glory. When these chains are broken, you will move from one level of glory to the next level of glory and so on and so on till infinity.

My pastor defines prosperity as getting to your destiny in the easiest and most direct manner. The Lord will embrace you with blessings. You will call people and show them what the Lord has done. This will happen if you acknowledge and accept that there is a spiritual dimension to entrepreneurship. We can ignore it but it is true. The question is which spirit will you listen to? The Holy Spirit or the spirit of our ancestors or other spirits advanced by others? The choice is yours. No one is going to twist your arm.

You know about business people who use charms or "muti" to advance their businesses or ventures. The good thing is that they realize that there is a spiritual dimension to business or doing business, the unfortunate thing is that they are turning to the wrong spirit for guidance. This is very common, it only comes out when the local newspapers pick it up.

God not only unshackles the chains of spiritual bondage but also gives you favour (Exodus 12: 35-36).

> "Now the children of Israel had done according to the word of Moses, and they had asked from the Egyptians articles of silver, articles of gold, and clothing. And the Lord had given the people favour in the sight of the Egyptians, so that they granted them what they requested."

It all starts from acknowledging the spiritual dimension of our ventures. The children of Israel were not only freed but also favoured with wealth as they left Egypt. The children of Israel lived in Egypt for 430 years but favour came in one day. Wow. From now going forward, generational curses will turn into generational blessings.

(Romans 8: 15) says

> "For you did not receive the spirit of bondage again to fear, but you received the Spirit of adoption by whom we cry out "Abba Father"."

When you are downtrodden in your business, at the height of the spiritual battle, remember help is on the way (Joel 2: 25-26).

> "So I will restore you the years that the swarming locust has eaten, the crawling locust, the consuming, the chewing locust, My great army which I sent among you. You shall eat in plenty and be satis-

fied, and praise the name of the Lord your God, Who has dealt wondrously with you, and my people shall never be put to shame."

(John 15: 16) says:

"You did not choose Me, but I chose you and appointed you that you should go and bear fruit, and that your fruit should remain, that whatever you ask the Father in My name He may give you."

Elijah repaired the altar that was broken, so too will the Lord repair your business. Restoration is coming. There is a spiritual battle that we have to fight. Make God your number one and you will be victorious in these spiritual battles. The joy of the Lord will be your strength. (Psalm 121: 1-2) says:

"I will lift up my eyes to the hills, from whence comes my help? My help comes from the Lord, who made heaven and earth"

It is your decision to let the Lord help. You are a decision away from your miracle.

During our spiritual battles, may we pray for an overtakers' anointing. May we not only be victorious but overtake our enemies. You might have started your business two months ago, but when the overtakers' anointing is on you, in your due season, you will overtake businesses that have been well established for over 20 years. The power of the Lord was upon Elijah such that he overtook, on foot, Ahab who was in a chariot on the way to Jezreel, (1 Kings 18: 46). Never look down upon the size and age of your business, when you have the overtakers' anointing; being small becomes immaterial. I am also praying for an overtakers' anointing as I write.

In 1996 I heard two people arguing at the work place. It was between a boss and a subordinate. I was amazed by the confidence of the subordinate. I think he could no longer hold what was in his heart. At the height of the vendetta the subordinate said something I will never forget up to this day. The boss said to the subordinate "I have a solid 20 years' experience in this job, and you should listen." I just stood there, mouth agape, astonished by the subordinate's reply. He said: "I do not care about your twenty years of destruction but my ten years of constructive experience."

We should pray for an overtakers' anointing. What you think is your strength might end up being your weakness. The number of years experience in your business or job, your qualifications. Let the joy of the Lord be your strength. He will hold your hand as you fight the spiritual battles.

May God preserve the inner man and have control over our soul. May the inner man and soul, see, feel and think beyond the natural.

When you have won the spiritual battle, do not forget The Lord your God. It is very clearly stated in (Deuteronomy 8: 1-20).

Chapter 7

WHAT IS SIN?

Sin is a potent or intoxicating mixture of desire and temptation. We should always desire for good things always. Good Godly desires. What you meditate upon from time to time and wish for becomes your desire. You really crave for it. It now becomes part of you. When given an environment to exercise flawed desires, the result is sin.

The formula of sin is,

Flawed Desires + Temptation = Sin.

If your desires are bad and flawed all you need to sin is just a dose of temptation. Sin is one of the reasons a lot of businesses do not prosper. There is a lot going on behind closed doors.

God will give you desires of your heart, good and flawless desires. Because Jesus quoted scriptures when He was tempted by Satan, it should encourage you to quote scriptures as well. Quoting scriptures might not work for you if your desires are flawed. We all know the desires of Jesus. They are also found in (Luke 4: 18-19). He was able to withstand the temptations because his desires were rooted in the word of God, which was why He quoted the scripture. It was not the quotes themselves that made him resist the temptations but the desires of His heart. Remember Jesus had just come from fasting, again this tells you a lot about His desires. What are your desires? Do you parrot cry verses when tempted, well sorry to disappoint you. That only comes natural if your desires are oriented towards the word of God.

Desires and temptations are ongoing. Make sure you maintain the right formula which is, Heavenly and Good desires + Temptation = No Sin. This can be applied to any situation, be it business or life in general. If you have mixed up desires and temptation comes, sin is the result. Temptations are ongoing as well. In (Luke 4: 13) it recorded that Satan, after tempting Jesus, only left Jesus for a season or left him until an opportune time. Temptations sometimes don't come directly as result of our choice but desires are.

As an established or aspiring entrepreneur, you should critically look at your desires. If you have good desires you will reap in abundance. Even when temptation comes you will overcome because your desires are good and facing in a different direction. If you have bad desires and temptation comes you will definitely succumb because your desires and the temptation are facing the same direction. We all know that the wages of sin is death.

Have you ever wondered how other people placed in the same tempting environment as you, resist? Is it that they are machines? No, they are human beings with feelings just like you and me. The reason why they don't succumb is the orientation of their hearts, in other words their **desires**. If your desires are mixed up, the chances of surviving in the business world, are very slim. I have observed the desires of many entrepreneurs just by chatting with them. One way you can tell is by observing a person's aspiration group(s). Aspiration group(s) is a term usually used by marketers. Look at the people they admire, you will observe that it's the wrong people altogether, even though they are popular people.

The end result of sin is death. Physical death, spiritual death and death to your business becomes inevitable.

Flawed Desires → Temptation → Sin → Death

Some entrepreneurs never grow. They are still the same that they were five years ago. It is not that they don't have a five year strategic plan document. You tend to ask yourself why this is so, until you are privileged to find out their desires, the orientation of their hearts.

Entrepreneurship is multifaceted. It's not bogged down to numbers only but goes as far as heart and mind issues.

A government can have good intentions of supporting its people through a multibillion dollar development loan facility. This can be either successful or futile. It depends on the desire of the recipient. I would urge governments to conduct DESIRE TESTS before they give out these loans. If you end up giving out a loan to someone whose desires are mixed up, the end result will be an automatic default once temptation creeps in. The leaders who want to give out the loans have good desires for you therefore you should match them with good desires of your own.

Let us put into practice what you have read. We have to build up one another in order to succeed in entrepreneurship.

(James 1: 12 – 18) explains how blessed one is that endures temptation. Once the bad desires have been conceived they give birth to sin. When sin is fully grown it brings forth death.

Chapter 8

WELL BALANCED GOALS – BALANCED DIET

Just as it is healthy to eat food that has protein, vitamins, carbohydrates, roughage, iron, so it is with a balanced diet of goals. Goals help one to focus productively into the future. Goals bridge the gap between where you are and where you want to be.

Most entrepreneurs set goals, which are only business and career related. Goals are multifaceted. When it comes to an enterprise you and your employees should all work toward shared and common goals. Simply announcing the goals to employees won't do the trick. There is an element of buy-in.

In a business set up goals have to be shared rather than simply announced. Employees have to buy into the goals. One managing director of a paint company noticed that there was a lot of wastage of raw materials in the factory. The factory workers saw the wastages as small and minor but if you quantify the losses it was substantial. He walked into the factory and started dropping US$10 equivalent notes. He pretended as if he did notice it. The factory employees started picking them up and ran to him, alerting him that he had dropped some valuable notes. The managing director's face beamed with delight as he turned ponderously towards the employees. He told them that the money he had dropped was equivalent to the value of raw materials on the factory floor, which they were ignoring, not picking up and wasting. He drove his point home. One the result of this was that the factory set a target of reducing wastage to almost 0%.

The managing director came up with a subtle way of getting a buy-in from the employees on one of the goals they had set for the factory. Simply announcing would not have done the trick. He got involved and earned a buy- in to the goal. A lot of managing directors, partners in firms and CEOs announce goals to the organization and expect that people will adhere to them. I have seen value statements like: "What we stand for". You will be surprised that the whole organization is going in the opposite direction.

From a broader perspective goals should include

1. Career Goals
2. Spiritual Goals
3. Personal Goals
4. Value Goals
5. Financial Goals
6. Healthy living Goals / Self Management Goals
7. Family Goals
8. Business Goals
9. Social Responsibility Goals
10. Result Goals

Knowledge is power. Breaking down of goals as above is powerful. Without knowledge, ideas are scattered but knowledge puts those ideas into perspective or in order, as shown in the diagrams on the next page.

Before being knowledgeable ideas and thoughts are scattered but after knowledge is imparted to you, your thinking pattern is more organized if not revolutionized.

You have to list all the ten goals and should have short range and long range goals. You will ultimately have ten short range goals and ten long range goals. Have a few goals under each item so that you don't have too many goals to pursue. Please write them down, don't leave them in your mind only. Writing them down somewhere will enable you to make an honest assessment of your achievements. When you reach some goals, celebrate. Give yourself a pat on the back. If you don't give yourself a pat on the back no one else will. When you don't succeed on others, don't give up. The good thing is that you know where to improve on. It is difficult to improve on something that you are not aware of. So write those goals somewhere so they will appear permanent.

The one that strikes me most are family goals. Although mostly neglected, in my opinion, it is one of the most powerful goals. Remember goals must be SMART – Specific, measurable, attainable, realistic and time-specific. KISS – Keep It Short & Simple. You don't have to be a genius and make it complicated. This equally applies to family goals. When and which school should the children attend? Which relative requires most assistance? How do you go about it?

When do you start and end this assistance? Everything has an ending, you know. The goals should not be too many, otherwise you might end up chasing the whirlwind.

Before Knowledge is imparted

```
   o      o              o
     o           o              o
  o
          o      o              o
     o
                    o
          o      o       o
```

After Knowledge is imparted

```
   o    o    o    o    o    o    o
   o    o    o    o    o    o    o
   o    o    o    o    o    o    o
   o    o    o    o    o    o    o
   o    o    o    o    o    o    o
```

Entrepreneurship requires that you be focused. Not adhering to, or having no goals, is like misreading signposts when you are driving. You know the consequences of this. It's a must to have a balanced diet of goals. Rich and great people have well defined goals that go beyond business and career goals.

Our school system should, mainly from primary school level, embrace the teaching of a balanced diet set of goals. These are steps that prepare us for the real world, which can be harsh sometimes. To be forewarned is to be forearmed. Book learning does not prepare us for the real world because in the real world, there are demons.

Setting goals and striving to reach them is powerful driving force. It can help to keep you out of trouble. It improves time management as well. You will enjoy healthy living. In achieving your goals, you must bear in mind that you are the most important resource. So take care of yourself. Without you, there are no goals to achieve.

One of the most powerful revelations of goals was made by a friend over a chat. He was thirty nine towards forty and I was thirty three towards thirty four. He made his goals at the age of twenty. He had a goal of marrying at a certain age (family goal), he said that he will buy a house at the age of thirty (financial goals). He also had a goal that he would start his own business at the age of forty (business goals). I could not stand but have admiration for this friend. He did get married at that age, bought his first house at the age of thirty-one, started his business at the age of thirty nine. Wow. He set his goals twenty years ago and followed them through. He was focused. The reason I mention this story is not only to tickle our fancy but also to assure you that you can make it as well. Sometimes a lot of people lack these basic inspirations and advice.

You can set your goals whilst young. Even if you are in your middle age or old age you can still set your goals. You will find that at certain ages some of the ten goals will be more critical and appropriate. Start today, where you are with what you have. If you don't have a pen, use a pencil, but start.

21-year-old Gabriel Kondesi in Malawi, who is believed to have done schooling only up to standard seven, started a community radio station from some equipment he assembled which included car batteries, a TV aerial, wires and a radio cassette player. This brilliant young man did not wait to see what other big players in the broadcasting industry were up to, he just started using the resources available to him in the village. He was not petrified by the success of these big players. He used these simple resources to impact on lives of his community of Mulanje by communicating important messages like weddings and bereavements. He is a promising entrepreneur and should be supported to realize his dreams.

My friend's goals were different from mine. I had no personal goals, my family goals were hazy and my financial goals were left in the hands of anybody who would employ me. Now that's dangerous living. Many of us are like that. Millions of us leave our financial goals in the hands of anybody who employs us. Have you ever heard of the term investing? Millions of us don't look beyond the pay cheque or pay slip. Employers are a platform for us reaching our financial goals. Suppose you work hard, upgrade yourself, you will get a promotion and improve your financial standing. When it's time to move on, it's time to move on in line with your financial and business goals.

Chapter 9

GOSSIP AND TIME WASTING

The tongue can be very dangerous. It can build and break relationships. You must maintain high levels confidentiality in clients' affairs. My friend said 'I keep my eyes open and my mouth shut'. Every client or customer has his / her own approach of dealing with issues. You duty is to offer guidance in line with the principles of best practice principles.

I almost laughed my lungs out when someone mentioned the word "grapevine" to describe word circulating within the offices. Now a certain gentleman did not know that this was a management term and said, "People are talking about grapevine all the time, next there will be lemon vine and orange vine." I trust now he knows the true meaning of what grapevine means from a business point of view.

Be open with people to reduce the likelihood of gossips in your business. Set a standard of how you tackle issues and be consistent and impartial. Once selective approaches are made it can kill your business. It is amazing the things that can destroy a business that is why I mentioned that entrepreneurship is multi-faceted. It's difficult to eliminate gossip in one's business but it can be greatly reduced. One can put up memos on the notice board on topical issues that affect operations and the livelihood of staff.

Gossip kills in that there is a lot of time wasting involved, time that could have been employed productively elsewhere. It can also de-motivate your staff. You might be asking how you are expected to remember all these things on entrepreneurship. Simple, they should become part of your values, your personal values. Walk the talk. It is not enough to announce a set of values to your employees while you don't personally live them.

When in leadership position, never be double minded, that is saying one thing and doing the other but believing in both.

If someone comes with some gossip to you, tell them your values regarding gossip. Educate them on how gossip destroys businesses and relationships. Some gossips can be very amusing but live your values. Don't be threatened or afraid that "juicy" information will pass you. That is one of our fears. We are afraid that something will hit us without us knowing. The only set-back is that once you entertain gossip, the more it comes and the higher the likelihood of you participating. Once you start participating you end up creating a tangled web for yourself because you end up defending yourself from accusations and defusing tensions. What a waste of time and intellectual capital!

Having lived in high-density housing areas, it is very common to see women chatting on their verandas. They can literally sit there from morning to evening chatting. This is something very common amongst housewives and non-working mothers. Widows are not spared in this practice. All this is precious time wasted. They talk about topical issues but live out issues that are sustainable that could put food on the table for a long period. This is very common in Africa. If that valuable time and energy could be put to good use, Africa would score good points. Is it that there are no projects for women to undertake? The result of running out of ideas is running out of money.

After chats, the other area often given priority is attending to lady functions like kitchen top-ups, baby showers, bridal showers, wedding parties and funerals. I am not saying it is bad to attend these functions but you will be surprised to find out how many people's calendar is filled with the above activities. This is constructive criticism. Norman Vincent Peale noted that the trouble with most of us is that we would rather be ruined by praise than saved by criticism.

These activities are taking over. People are mourning for five days the passing on of a beloved one. It is more important to do your best to someone during his or her living days than when one passes on. George S Patton, Jr. said that it is foolish and wrong to mourn the men who died. Rather, we should thank God that such men lived (Matthew 8: 22)

> But Jesus said to him 'Follow Me, and let the dead bury their own dead.'

Important business deals and meetings have been postponed because one has to attend the above mentioned functions. Sometimes it is wise to send people to represent you. Also look into investing in other activities that will sustain your future. Some business meetings are so important that depending on how you view them, they cannot be postponed. A major problem is the impression one creates in the minds of those who attend such meetings. It is quite a surprise for one to postpone a business meeting to attend a "baby shower". But it happens. You can attend both if you skilfully manage your time. You can communicate to those you are to a have meeting with, the time you will be available. It is good enough if your time at the meeting is limited but at least you attend the most important sessions of the meeting, then you can excuse yourself.

Imagine if we all were to attend all these social functions, would there be any business deals concluded during the weekend? Almost everyone has something else to do, especially members of a meeting. We have to realize that it takes a lot of sacrificing of competing of alternatives to attend a meeting, especially during the week end.

Men are not spared in how we sometimes spend our weekends. Men are natural breadwinners. This is not always so these days as some men are not taking their God-given positions in the home. Instead of planning how to ensure that one's projects are successful, some men are involved in a lot of non-value-adding activities. Some men have realized this and are often busy bees over the weekend. Unfortunately a lot of other men spend time clutching to bitter drinks and watching sports on public televisions. This is very common in Africa, be it in a fancy place or in a not-so-fanciful place. The issue is that time is moving and waits for no one. Time that is lost can never be recovered. I write this because if one million people in Africa could put a weekend to better use and avoid so many social activities, positive change could be the result.

If the weekend could be devoted to planning ahead of the following week and beyond, Africa would change. Planning ahead includes prayer because you would want God to guide you in your plans. Socializing is good but has to have limits especially if we live in a continent that is poverty-stricken. There is no time to waste. When our enterprises prosper, it means that we will have the capacity to employ more people. When more people are employed, ultimately absolute poverty becomes a thing of the past for the employees. For most of us, when we work, we do not take care only of ourselves and immediate family, but also our extended families and other relatives. If you get a job that pays well, you will be able to support or help your relatives in one way or another. If we can have one million people to plan ahead over the weekend, just think of how many people they can employ as a result of good planning.

Planning does not only happen from Monday to Friday but should also take place on Saturdays and Sundays. As we attend church over the weekend, let's plan to be better people and entrepreneurs. Let's think about our countries, our continent. A sum total of these thoughts can change the continent of Africa. This is not new in Africa. Moving from one country to another in Africa will improve your understanding.

It is painful to see how the poor and middle class spend their time over the weekend. The rich surprisingly are busy working out strategies for their businesses and investments. Just befriend one or two rich people and you will be amazed. I have observed how they spend their time, including weekends. Yes they will play golf. Have you ever visited them at their homes after playing golf? You will see an avalanche of books in front of them. This used to irritate me at first because I was being unproductive with my time and here is someone, who is already rich, and whom I admire, and he is busy writing something, or working on the computer. It is part of their lifestyle. It is true, look around, the people you interact with, that is you in five years time.

As long as gossiping and time wasting persist, the gap between the rich and poor will continue widening. After some time the poor will blame their government, environment, parents and friends for their state. What they don't realize is that it all started with a weekend where one wasted resources of time and money. Pleasure binges are not sustainable. These groups of people really do blame their governments. They point fingers at their leaders. Even if they were to be given a President of their choice, a good governance system devoid of corruption and that all that goes along with it, they would still remain poor. Still poor under ideal conditions, be careful when you criticize your leaders, if there was to be the change you requested, would you change yourself for the better?

Start now to spend your time wisely. Build your enterprises on a daily basis. Don't stop because the weekend has come, TGIF (thank God it's a Friday). The days of TGIF are over. Thank God for each day. On a Friday, relax and continue planning, even if it is one hour in the evening of Friday. Africa will not move out of poverty if we continue to sing the TGIF song. Other nations have done it, so can we, it starts with one person. Today's employees are tomorrow's entrepreneurs. So if you work and plan only from Monday to Friday as an employee, it will be difficult to stop this attitude as an entrepreneur.

Established entrepreneurs will tell you that they never cease working and planning. Therefore don't be an employee "EMPLOYEE", be an employee "PROSPECTIVE ENTREPRENEUR". You know as much as I do that there are employees who have declared their work places "no go areas" over the weekends, unless you lure them with some financial incentives. No one was born an entrepreneur; most entrepreneurs were themselves once employees. When blessings are coming and falling we sometimes look at who they are going to fall on, forgetting that those blessings can fall on you as well.

We are so used to looking around and listening to other people's testimonies and success stories. It is high time other people listened to your own success story. To achieve this we have to avoid time wasting activities regardless of which day of the week it is.

Chapter 10

WEAK LINK IN THE ORGANIZATION

Surprisingly some customers and clients try to look for a weak link in your organization. This is most common when they are negotiating a fee or price of a product. Every organization has got weak links but it is up to management to reduce the influence of weak links. That is true, even in the DMU of an entity, (Decision Making Unit).

It is very important to let everyone in the organization know that everyone there is a sales person of the company. They should be aware of the language when it comes to feeing or communicating the price. Once there are conflicting statements by two or more people in an entity, this signals danger to the customer and increases mistrust. Yes, some clients or customers do it deliberately in their quest to find a weak link. Once all personnel in the entity – from CEO, human resources, sales, marketing, production to quality control and so forth – embrace the idea that they are all salesmen and saleswomen, only then can you ameliorate the prevalence of weak links.

Just to be clear, you don't have to force it down their throats but you have to buy-in. You can only achieve this once all personnel have an ownership mind-set. Get them involved in various activities in the organization that foster this way of thinking. Remember "no involvement, no commitment." Be clear that when people make a mistake they should be open to correction.

Weak links in an organization take no particular shape, weight, colour, complexion, background or height. It can be anyone.

Chapter 11

THE BIG PICTURE

Whenever I have a discussion with a dear friend, he usually insists that one should look at the big picture. Finer details are important yes, but you will get to that later on but the big picture is more important. For example if one is going into the highway, you need to look ahead and concentrate on whether it is safe to proceed. Then you can proceed once it is clear or safe to do so and being mindful of which lane to take to get you where you are going. That is looking at the big picture.

You don't look and admire the other cars that are passing by, or stop to notice who is driving what, that is too much looking into the finer details. Yes you might eventually get to notice who is driving what once you are in the correct lane but that's not very necessary initially because you were looking at the big picture.

When giving out instructions to subordinates or employees make sure that you make them see the big picture as well. You have to see the big picture yourself in order to make someone else see a big picture as well. The problem comes when you, as the business owner, doesn't see things from a big picture view point. Tunnelled vision is very dangerous. If you have a tunnelled vision you will find it difficult to survive in the entrepreneurship world. The chances of giving up are high once events overcome you, once someone crushes your ideas to ashes. Try to see things from a holistic point of view. Then cascade these totals to finer details. Not the other way round. An optimist once said, "Where others see failure I see success"

Make it a point to make close friends with people who see things from a bigger picture point of view. This is the law of impartation at work. They should impart in you the skill of being able to see things this way. You have to work on it, it does not come naturally. This will be useful to both current and aspiring entrepreneurs. I have worked with brilliant people who are excellent in this area.

The one who stands out in this area is my former boss Alvin. He is a visionary. I have tried to master this skill. Young people should also start developing these skills. What we enjoy today, the high-rise buildings, nice cars, beautiful clothes, nice computers and so forth, was because some people were visionaries. Let's not spend time outliving today as though tomorrow will never come. We have to do something that our children's children will appreciate and praise us for.

When you are employed and join a successful company or business, you are actually there because someone looked at things from a big picture point of view in developing that company or organization. That person had a vision. The problem today is that there are too many people who see things from a smaller picture, they are tunnel vision minded people. It is these people that usually disturb people who see things from a broader perspective, the big picture minded people. Know who you are dealing with. Make an assessment of whether you are dealing with someone who looks at things from a big or small picture. Some people take static snapshots and don't move on.

When your clients or customers are not seeing the big picture, enlighten them. Once they are enlightened, the prospects of you making money are very high as long as your products or services fit their choice criteria. These are the advantages of seeing things and situations from a big picture view point. It can also earn you a promotion because you are seeing things that the boss is not seeing. When you are running your own business, make sure the board members or top management team is filled with big picture minded people without neglecting the finer details of course.

You need to work on acquiring the skill to see things from this viewpoint. It is a gradual process. You can tell whether you have matured to this state by your own words. How you participate in meetings and other discussions. No one will come and tell you that you have matured in this regard because not everybody knows where or how far you have come. I used to wonder why one person could be a board member of several companies.

When I read profiles of some people in the newspaper I used to be green with envy. Why do some guys have all the luck? I would question myself. It is not luck, neither is it necessarily hard work. These are mostly big picture minded people. When some people speak, you can predict their contribution, you can even anticipate in advance the depth of their contribution. It happens.

Problems should not hold you from seeing the big picture, when there is trouble it's an opportunity for God to show up.

Don't let people judge you with your present circumstance. Focus on the big picture. The God who watches over Israel, is watching over you. God is a God of big things. God has not abandoned his plans for you. He sees the whole big picture. Since we were created in his image, we too have the ability to think big and see the big picture.

Chapter 12

EXPAND YOUR MEANS

Don't live below your means or cut costs just to get by, no, you should expand your means by increasing your earnings to improve your bottom line, whether it applies to households or businesses. There is an easy way out and that is quitting. Although quitting is easy, it is not profitable. There are situations and mostly people who will make you think of quitting. Once you master the art of solving problems, your earnings will improve.

The unfortunate thing with most of us is that we want to be rich quick or at least in the shortest time possible. Although ideal, it is not also always so. This is because life is "a process of endless learning." If you sell goods you can prosper by reducing your gross profit, (GP%,) and push up volumes. Therefore your GP value per unit will be low but will be high in total when you sell huge volumes. Once the GP value is high enough you will be able to cover your selling, administration and distribution costs, (S.A.D).

If you are a service provider or into consulting, there is need to watch your efficiency or productivity. In consulting or providing services, you are mainly in the business of selling time. That is point number one. You need to remember this. This is so as you have to have standard charge-out rate. It does not need to be known by the client. You can estimate how long the job will take to complete and charge accordingly by multiplying your charge-out rate by the expected time required to complete the task. Always inform the client that this is an estimate in case there are some time overruns that are not of your own making.

Don't forget or be frightened to talk about disbursements. These are expenses at cost. You should be able to calculate your write-offs per job or client. This will help you in the learning process. You will need to reduce your discounts or write-offs to make more money. The higher the levels of discounts or write-offs the more you are working for free. Although adding value to others you are not doing yourself a favour.

That is why it is important to surge on and not quit but expand your earning capacity. There are marketing issues to be considered when calculating the above. That is where the 4 Ps come in. These four Ps are product, price, promotion and place (distribution). No matter how many Ps are added to the four basic Ps, the four are crucial. That is when your thoughts oscillate around these 4 Ps, you are a step ahead.

Never quit. Quitting is not an option when you want to get rich.

Chapter 13

BENCHMARKING

Benchmarking is basically comparing business performance with competitors or recognized leaders in the area or comparing against best practices or competitive practices. It is essential to obtain comparable relevant data. Benchmarking is also considered to be a quality assurance process.

Benchmarking has its own positives and negatives. Usually companies benchmark certain key indicators of their business against others in the same trade or industry, to establish whether they are within acceptable industry average. Comparisons can be made in the areas of quality, costs, accounting functions such as accounts payables or payroll and other specific processes. It involves identifying an entity that has a competitive advantage or quality over your company or business and try to match that or exceed it. This is very positive as you raise your standards of operations or quality. This applies to individuals as well, that is why people come up with role models, they are basically benchmarking.

Benchmarking slightly takes a negative turn when individuals over benchmark. Overdoing it can bring negative repercussions. You might benchmark your achievements to date against people who have "over achieved". This can be very frustrating as it could make you feel that you are way behind.

Catching up with the others might seem like a mere figment of your imagination. May be you trained your junior at work and that junior after a while is promoted and becomes your boss. You might have resigned from a particular job to take up another or start your own business but you find those whom you left behind are doing better in all aspects than you. You suddenly stop benchmarking against superior figures and companies or business and now focus on where you came from. The best advice is not to look back. Remember what happened to Lot's wife when she looked back, yes she turned into a pillar of salt. The Israelites spent 40 years in the wilderness because of disobedience, they started craving for the goodies in Egypt where they had come from. Don't look back. Engage those whom you left behind but don't look back, period. 'Never burn bridges because you might one day want to come back' – that is what the wise advice. It's true whether going back or not, NEVER BURN BRIDGES AT ALL.

This is so for the mere reason that you will need those people in the future, not necessarily to work for them but to leverage their experiences, intellect and so forth. The only bridges to burn are immoral and corrupt ones.

Benchmark wisely, benchmark against the best. Have you ever heard of 'Try, try and try again'. If you aim for something high, you are likely to exceed it, maybe match it, or slightly achieve less but if you aim for nothing be sure that you will get it.

From a business perspective you can benchmark some particular functions of your entity, for example accounts receivables or accounts payables. Basically you are benchmarking functions in the value chain, your key activities or problematic areas. Benchmarking can be done against a competitor or non-competitor, as long as they perform certain functions efficiently and effectively.

Benchmark is done against the industry's best practices. Watch the costs and output (results) of others and adjust accordingly. Sometimes your cost of producing items might be higher than your competitors'. There is a need to find out why your competitor is offering lower prices than yourselves, yet your business processes are almost similar. A quality circle can be tasked to look into this and implement its findings in relation to industry best practices. You can also benchmark against non-competitors as long as they perform certain functions better, effectively and efficiently.

A lot of companies engage in benchmarking. You should as well. Benchmarking is not necessarily an admittance of failure but simply a tool for ensuring that you maintain a competitive edge. It can be costly to your business if you are too late in benchmarking. Newspapers are good sources of what your competitors are up to. Some businesses like living in their own world. To be pragmatic we do not live in a vacuum. Do cross-company comparisons. You might find yourself out of business because of gross inefficiencies in a particular key business activity.

There are always areas for improvements even if you are doing well and achieving great margins. The issue is about sustaining those good results. They can be sustained by benchmarking. You can benchmark on how another company produces management accounts. An area to start is the planning period in relation to timing. Having worked for about five companies it is interesting to note how others plan very well to ensure that their management accounts are out in good time to enable management to take relevant decisions. Management accounts that are produced a month after the deadline might no longer be relevant because the world is changing fast. There is also an area of interest that companies should benchmark, this is the area of managing external audits.

One of the companies had an excellent program of managing external audits. It was able to coordinate very well its more than five divisions. It was a wonderful experience. Once we adhered to the timetable of producing what, and when, including receiving a phone call or two, you would find that all divisions completed the external audits by the set date. They would also include in the timetable dates when they would go for press release. It gave us a sense of responsibility because if you delayed any process it meant a delay in going to the press to release the group's results. Imagine if your division was the one responsible for the delay.

You can benchmark human resource issues with other businesses. This can be done in the following areas – recruitment, motivation, retention of employees, training and farewell functions for employees leaving the company. It reminds me of my boss in 1999 – 2001. She would buy us "small Christmas presents". There is no present that is really small; it's the thought that counts. It always kept me smiling and amazed. My late parents were committed at giving me presents during my birthday, my wife does as well. To expect such a benevolent gesture was touching and would ensure that one works harder than before.

Farewell functions or speeches that employers make when an employee is leaving are very important. In some companies, it's a tradition, a good tradition and should be encouraged. In other companies it is either non-existent or applied selectively. I have seen a friend walk out of the company on his last day on the job and that was all. I asked him over and over whether it was his last day in the company, even though I knew it was. It was a culture shock since I was about three months old at the company. I immediately knew what to expect during my stay there and I was right.

Once an employee leaves your company or business that person can be your goodwill ambassador. He or she can act as an advocate for your company. We sometimes come up with brilliant marketing ideas but miss the very small details, a farewell function. It doesn't have to be an expensive exercise. The boss has to turn up or appoint someone to represent him or her in the event of his absence. Some bosses go missing during these functions. These are areas to benchmark.

It is amazing to see how some people speak good things about their previous employers. It makes one want to buy their products or use their services because of their ambassadors. These advocates are not so because they received huge financial exit packages. Last impressions are as good as first impressions.

Even if the person who has left is a junior in the company, recognition is important. If the functions are expensive, because of their frequency, then you need to find out why there is a high staff turnover. Once resolved, the costs associated with these functions will drop. Mother Theresa when criticized that her benevolence would not save the whole world replied that without that drop of water in the ocean the ocean would be a drop less. Every gesture of goodwill matters. The sum total of these small gestures have far reaching positive effects. If you do not have that employee as an advocate of your company or organization, you have one advocate less in the pool of potential advocates.

There is a friend who vowed never to buy from a certain shop. Why, because when the employees knock off as late as 8-9pm, they are left to look for their own transport home. Transport in that area is difficult to find. Otherwise they have to hitch-hike from strangers to get to the point where they can find buses, if they are lucky. Such matters can be benchmarked because I have seen other setups or businesses provide some form of assistance to ferry their stranded employees. You can benchmark how they do it and emulate this at the lowest cost possible. Once you do this, at least you can win one customer back, customers and clients do pay attention to these finer details. My friend has a good and sound purchasing power.

You can engage consultants to carry out benchmarking activities for you. They don't have to mention the company or companies they are benchmarking against. There are some ethics that have to be observed when benchmarking.

In Africa, families or clans compare each other's successes. Sometimes it might end up violent. This should stop, it is not getting us anywhere as Africans. If a particular family is doing well in business or life in general, it is important to benchmark and emulate their success story. The comparisons are usually exacerbated by the elderly folks in the village. Once their son or daughter is doing very well in town they would go and tell or rather "show off" to their village friends whose children are not as successful. The best way to approach this if you are the recipient of such "good news", is to benchmark. Where did the children go right? How did the parents influence their successful children positively? It is never too late to promote your own children or clan. The success of others is not our defeat. Learn to benchmark. You might find out that this is free consultancy.

Chapter 14

WORRYING AND SORROW

Someone challenged that you could have invented or built the first cellphone if all your energies spent worrying was put to good use. Entrepreneurship is all about problem solving. When you solve a problem today, it prepares you to solver bigger problems tomorrow. There will be some sad and downward moments but you have to recover with haste. We all have peaks and troughs in our lives.

Sorrow will not solve your problems. Actually sorrow dims your vision. (Job 17: 7) says

> "My eye has also grown dim because of sorrow, and all my members are like shadows."

You can lose sight of what you want to achieve because of sorrow. You have no freedom when you are sorrowful. Sorrow causes you to stagnate. Sorrowing – yes, in its present continuous tense, causes poverty. Unending sorrow causes one to concentrate on how big the problem is and not how big God is.

Job's three friends initially came to comfort him but they ended up debating with him on the causes of his misfortunes. They showered him with pity and initially Job gave in by the change in his tone. Later Job held on to what he believed in until his restoration.

The joy of the Lord is our strength. Where there is no joy there is no productivity. Where there is no productivity there is no prosperity. Where there is no prosperity there is no fulfilment because we start blaming others for our present setbacks yet it all started with sorrow. It all started with us.

Sorrow is due to a number of reasons.

We worry mainly because we do not fully trust God to handle a situation. Replace your worries with prayer. Pray without ceasing.

The other cause of sorrow in business is that of opposing forces. You want to get somewhere but there seems to be something holding you back. You want to move from point E to J, but there are opposing forces and setbacks at point H. You want to get your desired net profit margin but overheads are growing beyond control. It is these opposing forces that you need to speak against.

One of the ways of overcoming sorrow is to always remember that you were made in heaven but assembled on earth. You are a product of heaven. Start declaring things, (Job 22: 28),

"You will also declare a thing, and it will be established for you."

Start saying

"I can do all things through Christ who strengthens me", (Philippians 4: 13).

Repeat this as many times as possible, in the morning, afternoon, evening, even just before you sleep.

Start declaring good things. Whatever you call your situation, it shall be. Adam was given the authority to name animals. (Genesis 2: 19):

... And whatever Adam called each living creature, that was its name.

When Adam saw a dog he declared it that it was a dog, when he saw a creature with a tall neck eating leaves he called it a giraffe. He declared the names and they were so. Start declaring that your business will be successful. Start giving your situation good names despite the odds. By worrying and sorrowing you will forget your address. Whatever you name your situation so shall it be. If you call it a hopeless situation, so shall it be. If you call it a hopeful situation so shall it be.

Entrepreneurship is not easy. Active entrepreneurs will agree with this. There are times you suffer and are grieved. This is the best time to start declaring things. Worrying and sorrowing will not add value to you, your business and situation at hand.

Focus on new beginnings when your business does not work out. Our God is a God of new beginnings. (Genesis 1: 1):

In the beginning God created the heavens and the earth.

If God is a God of new beginnings and you were created in his image, it means that you are also a person of new beginnings, new and positive beginnings.

Chapter 15

LEARN TO SEE OPPORTUNITIES

Opportunities do not just come knocking on the door. You must be able to identify them. Good opportunities present themselves in various forms. Your eyes need sharpening, metaphorically speaking. Let me ask you and tell you a secret at the same time. When you read the newspaper, what do you like reading? Is it politics, the favourite of many?

When one reads the newspaper, one should not just read it for the sake of amusement but look for opportunities. Not job vacancies, the obvious opportunities. There are many opportunities in a newspaper more than you can ever imagine of. I laugh when I see people reading a newspaper thoroughly. I often wonder whether they have an exam the following day concerning that newspaper.

One difference between the rich and poor is what they see when they read the same thing. A rich man will see opportunities and the poor man will see stories and current events. Therefore the rich become richer and the poor poorer. The mere fact that they are rich does not necessarily mean that they automatically have the financial muscle to take advantage of opportunities. There are some things that money can't buy.

Usually we give up and point out that "If only I had money". I want you to look at the newspaper differently from now on. The small cash you use to purchase a newspaper can bring you a life changing opportunity. That is a big secret that people don't know. There are opportunities from the front page to the back page. May be we should have a test or exam on opportunities identified. Try to write down on a piece of paper at least ten opportunities that you have identified. You don't need to be highly educated to take advantage of opportunities. Continue writing them down every time you buy a newspaper. The more you do this, the more your art of searching for opportunities improves. Next time there will be no need to write them down but simply know them as you read the newspaper. There are a lot of business opportunities in newspapers. Just put on your X-ray eyes, metaphorically speaking.

Apart from newspapers opportunities will present themselves differently. We were going to have a married couples' dinner on one Friday. A number of church members were asked to sell the dinner tickets. It was not going to be easy. It was not going to be easy sell, let alone generate the enthusiasm to sell the dinner tickets. Something dawned on me as I began selling the dinner tickets. I saw it as an opportunity to improve my selling skills, an opportunity to come up with a sales pitch, sell the benefits rather than just selling the card, opportunity to improve my communication skills, opportunity to make new contacts, opportunity to make new friends, opportunity to serve. When I took the challenge as an opportunity, I sold many tickets.

From all this you don't know who will be your next employer or business partner. All the opportunities highlighted did not seem obvious but I just had to identify them. Those who did not volunteer to serve by selling tickets missed out all these opportunities because all they saw was selling of tickets. I saw more. The glass was half full and not half empty. Volunteer to serve, there are great opportunities in service.

When opportunities are identified, they should be grabbed. I am talking about moral and ethical opportunities. Do not wait for the outcome of another event to determine whether you should grab the opportunity at hand now or later. Procrastination is a killer. Events don't always move in juxtaposition. Sometimes the positive outcome of a particular event will be realized after months or years, therefore you can't postpone an opportunity at hand. You have to run with patience. Run and grab the opportunity at hand, make hay whilst the sun shines. After realizing the above, I have made it a point to be wiser as far as opportunities are concerned.

I phoned up the secretariat of where I am a director and board member, informing them that I would like to seek permission from the board chair to attend a one-day course by the Institute of Directors, as long as there was funding available. Well the response was not very encouraging. They reckoned that since elections for a new board were in three months' time, I might no longer be a director in the fourth month, depending on the outcome of the elections at the AGM. I saw an opportunity to advance myself and add value to the organization.

Learn to see opportunities

Well my response was exactly as I have written above. Never wait for the outcome of something to grab an opportunity as hand. Don't postpone.

There are also opportunities to give. Opportunities to give include tithes, love offerings, vow offering and so on. We have love auctions at church as a fund raising activity. It usually happens after the sermon towards the end. Food items such as apples, bananas, cakes, scones and drinks are auctioned. When the auction, which takes about 20 minutes, is over, the food is shared amongst everyone present – whether you contributed to the auction or not. Wow. The sad thing is that some people leave the church as soon the sermon is over and don't participate in the auction.

My wife participates in baking some buns, out of sacrifice, even when we have very little at home. After presenting the food, it is not known who cooked what. After contributing towards the baking I would have no money in the pocket to participate in the auction, maybe like other members. The good thing is that I will usually stay put and be myself and wait for the opportunity to eat. I feel for those who left just before the auction for two reasons. One is that this is an opportunity to give. Secondly it could be an opportunity to get your healing after eating fresh fruits. We complain about stomach aches and pains but we miss opportunities to get healed.

God is only asking you to see opportunities. Like I said opportunities also come indirectly; they are not always direct. We miss opportunities in many ways. I pray to God that He helps me to see opportunities, including the ones that are not always obvious. I encourage you to pray the same as well. Some people see God in US$1 or 1 British Pound, it is better than not seeing God in US$100 000 or 100 000 British Pounds.

Some opportunities are also direct. In (1 Kings 3: 5) it is recorded that when Solomon was at Gibeon, God asked Solomon to make any request and He would fulfil it for him. Solomon asked for wisdom; he asked for a wise and discerning heart. God was pleased with Solomon because he asked for something that would enable him to execute his duties efficiently as king. He was also given riches and honour. What would you have asked if the same happened to you today? Would you ask for a fancy car, a beautiful house, the latest fancy computer? Be honest, in your answer.

To become an entrepreneur you have to prepare yourself and go through some processes. Most entrepreneurs were once employees. I have seen many employees crying that they earn too little. I believe this is one of the biggest complaints of an employee, "I don't get enough money as I should or deserve." This was also my song before I came to some realization that I was singing the wrong song.

Instead of asking or begging your employer to increase your salary why not beg the employer to develop you? Ask the employer to send you to short courses and possibly long-term courses like diplomas and degrees. Ask the employer to give you more challenging work if you feel your current work is not challenging enough. Ask your employer to participate in the multi-skilling exercise at your company.

Multi-skilling would basically be moving from one department to another to gain skills in other areas of the organization. The department you might work in for one month before you are moved to the next might not be directly related to your field, for example a financial accountant working in the quality control department for one month. The point I am driving at is that you should not ask to be given the fish all the time, ask to be equipped with skills of how to catch fish. There are deafening silent cries for salary increases. Yes we need money, more money to meet the ever increasing cost of living. The problem is, what do we do when the money does not come our way after exhausting all options? That is why you see gloomy faces early in the morning. When you reach this point, better still before you reach this point, explore ways of being equipped by the employer to prepare you for greater challenges.

As mentioned earlier, attending short courses that sharpen your brain is one way. Participating in the multi-skilling exercise at the workplace is another. If multi-skilling is not there at your workplace, propose that it be introduced. Remember you have creation in you, because you were made in the image of God, The Creator. Who knows you might end up being the Chief Executive Officer of the company because you have been exposed to all the departments in the organization. Our focus should not be on the boss but the work, which we are doing. We need to look at where we are going, rather than focus on the multiple problems of employer-employee relations.

If you are dissatisfied by one employer and move to another, you will think you are moving for greener pastures but will be surprised to find the grass there scorched. Every workplace has its own type of problems; the most important thing is whether you solved your own problems. Ask to be taught how to catch fish so that you can catch as many as possible in future. Learn the ropes, get the techniques, that is the beginning of entrepreneurship. Crying for money will not always solve problems, learn to see opportunities.

The problem with many of us is that we feel these things apply to others and not to us. This is all psychological, it's just meant to make me feel good. With this mindset we will never move forward. If you ask successful entrepreneurs, they will tell you exactly what I have mentioned above. You can have someone who is a class A mathematical genius struggling to be an entrepreneur while someone who only reached the sixth grade being successful. They have learnt to see such opportunities. As mentioned in the introduction, entrepreneurship is multi-faceted and not intricate. King Solomon did not ask for gold or silver from God, but he asked for Wisdom. King Solomon knew that with wisdom it would enable him to have gold and silver.

Remember to remember that your prayer has been answered. Your good days are coming. The answer might not be direct, perhaps not in the manner you exactly want it to be but indirect. God does not throw away prayers, therefore never cease praying; the answer is on its way. Pray for the discernment of opportunities.

One area we miss opportunities is that of financial discipline, in particular hotel bills. The company I worked for had presence in four countries in Southern Africa. The four divisions would have quarterly management meetings in a host country. Guess what, our financial discipline and prudence was evident in our hotel bills. It was an indicator to management of how financially disciplined we were in our own countries. It was shocking to hear how some individuals would load their hotel bills with costs from the bar. The bill would have high beverage costs. My boss and I were subtle, any side bills we met the expenditure from our own personal pockets. We never heard our names mentioned in the corridors of head office as we maintained strict financial discipline.

When hosted by someone in a hotel whether you are an employee, entrepreneur, aid worker, charity organizer and like, never abuse the privilege that someone else is paying the bill. This is an opportunity to show your financial discipline. Like I said, some opportunities do not come directly. If you load your host with unnecessary expenditure, this sends some cues to him or her about you. Even if your host says, "enjoy, I will pay for everything, the bill is on me", beware and just spend on accommodation itself, laundry and meals. The meals should not be inclusive of other guests' meals, there is a temptation to invite friends and relatives and sing "come and see what the Lord has done." If you must invite them, you must pay for them from your own pocket. It is not a good thing for one person to be indicating a meal for two or more people. This shows total financial indiscipline. It not only shows financial indiscipline but also that you are a consuming person. Your consuming mentality becomes very evident. Your principals are looking for a producing leader and not one with a consuming mentality. It is strange how all this comes out in just a simple hotel bill. We all know that this is happening.

Let us build up one another, you might be surprised why a promotion is taking time to come, why the business deal is being delayed, why you are not being assigned to another country on a special mission. As Africans, how are we going to add value to our own raw materials if we have a consuming culture? It is time that we change to a producing culture, for the sake of our children's children, for the sake of the future generations of Africa. Small things like hotel bills matter a lot, they send cues about how disciplined you are financially. Rich people know these indicators, the poor are not so privileged with this information. I have been hosted in hotels and we have hosted people in hotels and I see it happening.

It is not so much about the size of the bill but the items charged to the bill, the cues that are attached to the bill. It is true that the host can meet the expenditure but watch out for the cues that the bills send. I am not stopping you from having that roasted chicken you love so much but watch out for the cues that the bill sends.

You might be wondering how the office will know. If it is the Chief Executive Officer or Finance Officer responsible for your bill, it means he has to sign on the hotel bill before the accounts department pays for it. In the process of authorizing payment, the CEO or FO wants to know what he is signing for. That is when he really gets to know you. If he saw you as a responsible person, the contents of your hotel bill will now put some doubt in his mind. This is because of your own making. Anyway it is never too late to change, now that you know you should be more cautious in future. When being hosted or accommodated it is an opportunity to show that you are financially disciplined. "Small" things keep us in poverty or stagnation.

(Proverbs 22: 7) says

"The rich rule over the poor, and the borrower is servant to the lender."

Life is full of opportunities. When a country's debt is cancelled by the lender, it is not a time of unending celebration. It is a relief, yes. When a debt is cancelled it means that you have failed to repay the lender. When the lender gave you the funds he or she expected you to do well and be in a position to return the funds plus interest. Unfortunately as a borrower you are not doing as well as expected and therefore cannot meet your loan obligations. Therefore when the debt is cancelled, it is an opportunity to consider your ways. It should trigger deep reflections.

Sometimes we have our debts cancelled by one lender and then use that relief or cancellation to go and borrow from another lender. I have been there myself, so I know how it works. The "new" lender will ask you, who you currently owe and you declare that there is no one. The prospective lender will do his or her own investigations and find out that it is true that you do not owe anybody else. Equipped with the finding, the "new" lender will lend funds to you with an expectation that you will return it plus other charges.

We have used the cancellation of a debt to borrow more. You cannot destroy a bad habit by cultivating another. This applies to individuals, families, businesses, countries and nations. When a debt is cancelled, before celebrations begin, first of all let's consider our ways. A simple five-year or ten-year strategic document will not do unless we consider our ways. The input to the strategic document is all learned, people have diplomas and degrees on how to prepare such documents. Unless we as individuals consider our ways will remain servants of the rich.

Chapter 16

REBUKE MEDIOCRITY

God never created us to lead a mediocre life. At least not me, I rebuke mediocrity from today onwards. God created us with creativity in us, to be people of influence and purpose. It sometimes just takes you to say, "enough is enough"

A mediocre life is a life of half here, half there. This will not get you anywhere. Mediocre people have no competitive advantage. They have no extra edge over situations. Be a go-getter. I wonder if there are any business owners or shareholders who would accept mediocre results for their businesses. If not, then why lead a mediocre life? You are simply not going to add value to anyone or any business with mediocrity. You are always happy to go along with what is already there.

Go-getters, and not the mediocre, seek greener opportunities to make a difference. One can sacrifice a current job in search of more challenging roles. Challenging jobs have their own rewards, sometimes they might not be clear but they are there.

Companies do not need mediocre Chief Executive Officers (CEOs), otherwise you will end up being a Creator of Every Obstacle. Neither are mediocre Finance Director (FDs) needed, otherwise there would be serious financial problems. Mediocre doctors are also not very helpful as well, you know what would happen to the patients. In whatever discipline you are, never have a mediocre approach to things, it only delays, if not deter progress. As an entrepreneur, make sure you hire the right people in your organization, otherwise if it is full of mediocre individuals, you will only achieve mediocre results.

A story is told of a hunter who picked up an eagle's egg one day during his hunting adventure. He took the eagle's egg and put it in the chicken run for a hen to give warmth so that it could hatch it. After the egg hatched the eaglet grew amongst the chicken. It tried with frustration to do what the other chickens were doing. One day the eaglet saw a big eagle flying high in the sky. It was so magnificent in the eyes of the eaglet. It asked the mother hen what that beautiful creature, that flew so high, was. The mother hen told the eaglet never to look that way up again and to stop admiring the flying bird but just concentrate on the life in the chicken run where the eaglet was stationed.

That story is just what leading a life of mediocrity is like. A lot of people have silenced us when we wanted to fly and be superstars. Unfortunately we have given in and let them win. We have since then continued living a life of mediocrity, a half-and-half life. We might have been hatched in the life of mediocrity but its time to get out of it. You too can fly high like that beautiful eagle. We were created to shine and fly high. Failure to do so, means that we will always be clapping hands for other people's success. Time is up, people should now start clapping hands for our achievements in our enterprises.

One of the dangers of mediocrity is debt. The middle class is always in danger of being in perpetual financial debts. When you step out of mediocrity you will find out that the financial implication is bidding farewell to debt. There are some rich people and above average people who refuse to take loans from the banks despite numerous offers. When you try to look at the common factor in these individuals you will discover that they are always in pursuit of excellence. The words average or mediocre do not exist in their vocabulary.

When running your own business, always pursue excellence and you will always escape the mediocrity trap.

There are many African songs glorifying poverty or talking about how poor one is. Some radio stations play these songs quite often. Songs that tell us how one has suffered or is suffering. We need to sing a new song. These songs have entrenched poverty as part of our lives. I refuse to accept this thought pattern. I rebuke such songs that glorify poverty. Poverty is not part of anyone's lifestyle, neither is it part of anybody's culture. I hope the radio stations will refuse to play of such songs that talk about how one has suffered or is suffering. Mediocrity must be rebuked if we are to get out of the poverty trap.

Chapter 17

TRANSFORMATION A MUST

What good is good advice if it does not lead to transformation? Transformation only comes after renewing of the mind. (Romans 12: 2)

"And do not be conformed to this world, but be transformed by the renewing of your mind, that you may prove what is that good and acceptable and perfect will of God"

When the men and women of God preach to us, the pastors, priests, elders, deacons, they do not do so just to make us feel good. It is not to make us have a "feel-good" sense but to transform us. If we are not transformed by the word of God, the laws made by men will reform us and that doesn't sound nice.

Transformation basically means change. You have to change the way you perceive things, treat your employees, customers and peers. Transformation can also mean leaving behind of **excess baggage**. You don't need some unnecessary weights. These could be unproductive friends, acquaintances, meetings, habits and some relationships. Is the bottle half full or half empty? When you are transformed you start seeing things from a positive angle.

Transformation is key to being a successful entrepreneur. It unlocks a lot of potential. Without transforming your own life, how can you transform a business's misfortunes to fortunes? Those who have achieved business turnarounds will tell you how they transformed their lives first. Rotarian Hebert J. Taylor created the Four-Way Test in 1932. It has been translated into more than 100 languages. He introduced the four-way test in the cookware company in order to change the way people perceived things. Rotarians have adopted and applied the four-way test in their businesses and professional lives.

The Four-Way Test states that:

Of the things we think, say or do

1. Is it the truth?
2. Is it fair to all concerned?
3. Will it be beneficial to all concerned?
4. Will it build goodwill and better friendships?

The above led to total transformation within the company. He virtually changed the ethical climate to Club Aluminium. All levels of the organization started working with unity of purpose. Soon the company became profitable and cash flows improved. There was no need to liquidate the company anymore. They were transformed by the renewing of their minds. He died in 1978 but the 4-Way Test lives on and has impacted on millions of people's lives. You can also transform your business as well. If you are starting a business, start it with a transformed mind. You will surely reap the positive results.

The four-way test goes hand-in-hand with the Greek philosopher, Socrates' 'Test of Three Cups'. The three cups are that of truth, goodness and usefulness. You should check your facts whether they are true, not hear-say, you should ensure what you say about other people is good, and useful. If what you plan to say does not pass these tests, then there is no need to say it.

Mark Twain said, "when in doubt, tell the truth."

Time should transform you as well. Learn to learn from your past mistakes and success. Repeat your success and not your mistakes. You must progress as you grow older, growing in wisdom and deed. This is very important in entrepreneurship, if you do not grow yourself, how do you expect your business to grow? You must progress with time as the years go by. Be transformed and change for the better. I was stuck to the profit and loss or income statement issues for the first eight years of my working career. I progressed on to the balance sheet in the next six years. Now I am exposed to both the profit and loss account as well as the balance sheet. To me this is progression, if not success.

I make meaningful contributions when people discuss their financial statements. It was a dream I had to be exposed to the balance sheet at work. Now I rub shoulders with renowned entrepreneurs. During the years I was focused on the 'profit and loss', , I always felt intimidated when people discussed the 'balance sheet', using technical terms like equity, net worth, return on capital employed, debt / equity ratio and so forth. I knew them theoretically but that was all, the real world is about application and not only theory. Theory will win you admiration but not necessarily money. I am a transformed man and still learning. Learning doesn't end, it becomes exciting when those little detached pieces start coming together. You just have to have the right mindset and attitude to embrace change.

Chapter 18

HUMILITY PAYS

You might get away with pride for now but it won't take you very far. There was an army commander by the name of Namaan, (2 Kings 5: 1-19), who initially let pride rule him but realized that his leprosy was not going to be healed unless he set aside his pride and humble himself.

Namaan who served under the king of Syria was a great and honourable man. His only hope was a prophet in Samaria. "Then Namaan went with his horses and chariot, and he stood at the door of Elisha's house. And Elisha sent a messenger to him, saying, "Go and wash in the Jordan seven times, and your flesh shall be restored to you, and you shall be clean." But Namaan became furious and went away and said, "He will surely come out to me, and stand and call on the name of the Lord his God, and wave his hand over the place, and heal the leprosy."

Wow. Namaan wanted the healing to take place his way. It's my way or the highway approach. This was a wrong approach to the situation at hand. God's ways are not our ways. Pride had taken over when humility was all that was required. As you will find out, Namaan almost missed his healing, so too can you miss your blessings if you are not willing to humble yourself before others. You might have had a head start, maybe through inheritance, but there are some people who have gone ahead of you. Let's learn the good from them.

What made Namaan too proud? :

- He was a commander of the army. This was a position of power and influence. It was not a position for the faint hearted but the brave.
- He had direct access to the King. This is just like you having direct access to the President or Prime Minister of your country.
- He led victorious battles
- He was a mighty man of valour

- He had servants at his house
- The king listened to Namaan. Imagine a President or Prime Minister taking your advice. The King of Syria wrote a letter to the king of Israel.
- He was rich. Namaan took with him ten talents of silver, six thousand shekels of gold, and ten changes of clothing.
- He had audience and access to kings of other nations. Namaan brought the letter to the king of Israel. It's just like you having audience and access to Presidents and Prime Ministers of other countries.

It can be clearly seen why Namaan was too proud. Namaan asked, "Are not the Abanah and the Pharpar, the rivers of Damascus, better than all the waters of Israel? Could I not wash in them and be clean?" So he turned and went away in rage.

The good thing about Namaan is that he was a good listener. He was a listening boss. Other bosses only listen to themselves. They only hear the sweet melodies of their voices. When a business starts failing then they start calling for strategic planning meetings. It is important for people who hold responsible posts to listen to others for their own good and for the good of others.

Namaan's servants convinced him to listen to Prophet Elisha. Namaan later on humbled himself and dipped seven times in the Jordan and his flesh was restored like the flesh of a little child and he was clean. Humility pays. He had to forget all issues concerning his seniority, wealth and influence. Humility is a key to long-term and sustainable success.

Namaan's healing was permanent and not temporal. He put aside his pride and humbled himself. Everyone in business and life craves for long-term success. Don't worry about who is watching you. Humility is not a weakness, a belief that the world has. It actually gives you ample time to think things over and act rationally. Namaan must have been embarrassed to dip himself in the River Jordan as his servants must have been watching him. When you are about to receive your breakthrough, you do not mind who is watching you. You start defying protocol and decorum.

It has been mentioned earlier about being a good listener. Saul lost his kingship because he did not listen to God. When he went to attack the Amalekites he spared the best of the sheep, the oxen, the fatlings, the lambs, against God's commands (1 Samuel 15: 1-34).

> "Now the Lord said to Samuel, "How long will you mourn for Saul, seeing I have rejected him from reigning over Israel? …"

By the print of these words, may God not reject me and my future plans. There was nothing Saul could do now for God had rejected him. May God not reject you as you enter the entrepreneurship arena. Pray a prayer of repentance and ask God not to reject you from the on-set. Sometimes we wonder why things are not moving from the on-set. Let's learn to listen to God's voice. I know that you are asking how you can hear God's voice. I have asked myself and other people this question many times.

You can hear God's voice through visions or dreams, through other people, situations. There is always a voice inside you that tells you the right things to do although most often we decide not to listen to it. Things were not working in one of the companies that I worked for. Since I was second in command, my voice carried some power. The first in command and I started questioning each other, why we were not making progress. We resolved that prayer power was needed. We were both stunned as we had exhausted all laid down strategic options and resolved that prayer was the next strategic option we would take. Every morning at 8am all staff members met for quick briefings on the progress and plans we had. We gave each person tasks for the day. The meetings only lasted a maximum of 10-15 minutes. We started with a prayer. The prayer lasted for 1 to 2 minutes.

Things started changing for the good. Relationships improved greatly, no more office politics and gossip. Sales grew. Ideas started flowing in. Cash flows improved. Some promotions came along. Facilities to buy plots, land, cars started being available. Any staff of this company is my witness. God had not rejected us, He heard our cries to him. There are times, places and situations when our own intelligence is clearly insufficient for the task at hand. God will start taking over once we **humble** ourselves before Him and ask him to take over. I think now you are starting to realize how multi-faceted business is. A business has many dimensions to it and this book seeks to explore those areas often ignored.

Chapter 19

MAN LOOKS ON THE OUTSIDE

The anointing of David came as a surprise to his father and brothers. This was so because he was the least expected to be the future king of Israel. He was the youngest and merely looked after sheep. (1 Samuel 16: 7)

> "But the Lord said to Samuel, "Do not look at his appearance or at his physical stature, because I have refused him. For the Lord does not see as man sees; for man looks at the outward appearance, but the Lord looks at the heart."

This was after Samuel thought Eliab, one of Jesse's son, was the anointed one.

Man looks on the outside, that includes your dressing or appearance. This can be unfortunate but if you look at the flip side, you can turn it to your advantage. How you present yourself is extremely important. You are not dressing to necessarily impress but you are dressing for success. That is all to it. When someone mentions your name, an impression comes into their mind of how you look like. In other words, a visual impression of you comes into their minds. May they visualize a well dressed you. A bad visual impression might deny you business prospects.

Just try it. Call someone you know by phone and ask them whether they visualized you when they started talking to you. When I realized this power, I started dressing smartly and appropriately at various functions. Other people may say there are some informal gatherings, well let me be the judge of that. That's partly why some people may remark that , ' "Mr A or Ms B left a great impression". What they mean is that when they visualize you, all they see is, good. Remember we are all beautifully and wonderfully made by God. Radiate that beauty.

Chapter 20

GOD HAS A PLAN FOR YOU

Israel was run by judges during the days of Samuel, until the elders of Israel gathered together and asked for a king to rule over them. (1 Samuel 8: 1-22).

> "Then all the elders of Israel gathered together and came to Samuel at Ramah, and said to him "Look, you are old, and your sons do not walk in your ways. Now make us a king to judge us like all the nations." God granted them their request, verse 22.

There arose a vacancy for a king but who was going to fill it?

God chose Saul, son of Kish, to be king. How it happened truly amazes me. It all started with some lost donkeys. A journey in search of lost donkeys led Saul to being anointed king of Israel. Kish, Saul's father, had lost some donkeys. So Kish asked Saul to go and look for the lost donkeys. He also asked Saul to take one of the servants with him.

They passed through many mountains and places but did not find them. Saul had given up and wanted to return so his father would not start worrying about him. Then the servant advised Saul that there was a man of God in the city, who could show them the way to take. Saul told his servant that they had nothing to give the man of God since they had run out of food. The servant told Saul that he had one-fourth of a shekel of silver with him. The servant said that he would give it to the man of God.

So they went to the city where the man of God was. After enquiring from the young women who had gone out to draw water, they were told of the sacrifice that was going to take place in the city. The man of God had to bless the sacrifice first before the people could eat it. Surely they would find him before he went up to the high place to eat.

So they went up to the city. In the city they met Samuel. Samuel had been told by God that around the same time, He was going to send a man from the land of Benjamin and he would anoint him as commander over Israel. God told Samuel that the man would save Israel from the Philistines for He had heard their cries. Wow.

When Samuel saw Saul, the Lord revealed Saul to him. Saul asked Samuel where he could find the prophet and Samuel revealed himself. Samuel immediately invited Saul to eat with him. Samuel told Saul not to be anxious about the donkeys he had lost three days before for they had been found. Saul was amazed at the good things that the prophet said about him and his father's household.

Saul in his amazement reminded Samuel that he, Saul, came from the smallest tribes of Israel, and that his family was the least of all the families of the tribe of Benjamin. They went on to sit in the place of honour to eat together with the other invited guests. Wow from missing some donkeys to sitting in a place of honour with a man of God and about thirty invited guests. What an about-turn of events.

Saul actually had a big portion of meat reserved for him. Saul must have been overwhelmed, I would have been too. So Saul ate with Samuel that day. The following day Saul was anointed with oil as commander over Israel. Later Saul was proclaimed King of Israel. The first King of Israel.

God has a plan for you. This was a man who was sent to find some lost donkeys and yet ended up being proclaimed as the first King of Israel. In our pursuits of both life and business we reach a point where we believe that our prognosis is 90% failure. Either you are making huge losses or there has emerged a new very aggressive competitor. The most inviting option may be to simply give up. But let me tell you today, that God has a plan for you. The story of Saul is rejuvenating. Some of us haven't lost much but we only face tough times and we want to give up. The donkeys that Kish lost, were part of his wealth. To have some servants then meant he had some reasonable wealth.

Some people wait and say God is going to bless them. They will spend time praying and not acting on anything. Not also listening to the advice of others but waiting to hear the voice of God. Yet God has placed some people in our lives to take us to the next level of glory. Some entrepreneurs do not like help from anyone because to them it constitutes inadequacy. A lot of people want to go it alone. Actually a lot of us are like the rest of us. God has really placed some people in our paths so that they can be a blessing to us.

Saul took along his servant. The servant was an employee in Saul's household. Later on it was the servant who encouraged Saul not to give up when he wanted to return to his father's house. It was the same servant who had information about the man of God. It was the same servant who had silver to present to the prophet. It is good that Saul was humble enough to take his servant's advice and offer otherwise he would have missed his kingship. One would have thought that since Saul was the master, he would be courageous and have a persevering attitude and would also be the one to have silver or gold. But it was not so.

Exactly my point, the least people you expect to help you are sometimes the people who help you the most. I now never look down upon anyone otherwise I might miss my kingship. You don't have to take bad advice but good advice.

What you think is a disaster or calamity can turn out to be a blessing. It all depends on your attitude towards the problem at hand. You can move mountains with the right attitude. Your attitude determines your altitude. (Philippians 2: 5) says:

> Let this mind be in you, which was also in Christ Jesus

If you have a bumpy start in your business endeavours, you should have the right attitude not give up. Keep on looking for the donkeys. Remember who owns the cattle on thousand hills. When you are hungry and downtrodden ask God to slaughter one cow for you. The reason I write this is to position you rightly in the way we see problems. Move on, keep at it. Saul and his servant moved across many mountains. They sweated a lot. It wasn't easy looking for donkeys without binoculars.

There will be some perspiration before you reach your next level of glory. A lot of people want things the easy way. Even some wives or husbands like to seat back and relax while the other partner sweats it off at work. These things are happening. "No sweat, no sweet." When we see some people being successful, we end up being jealous and would not want to celebrate with them for their success. Learn to celebrate your friend's victories as if they were your own. This should be an encouragement that hard work, and not laziness, pays. Others start cursing the successful. You were not born to be poor. Therefore you should buy that beautiful car and dream house. The late nights would have paid off.

When you are not sure which direction to take, ask those who know. Yes consult others. There is no one with a monopoly of knowledge. We all need to ask when we are not sure. It is part of the research process. The information which you receive is no longer the other person's but now yours. That's how we become knowledgeable. Wisdom comes from God. Wisdom gives you a competitive advantage over the knowledgeable. Grace plus knowledge will lead to wisdom.

Saul and the servant enquired from the young women who had gone to draw water on the whereabouts of the man of God. The young women had the exact details. Marketers will tell you the importance of market research or market intelligence, which is part of the marketing information system (MIS).

Never look down upon yourself. You might have come from the countryside or village to town but God has a plan for you. You might not have an address but God will give you an address. You might have no sweet song but God will give you a new song. Never look down upon yourself or your business. A journey of a thousand miles starts with a single step. The corporate giants were once just an idea. The idea was screened and later actualized. They grew from strength to strength with visionary leaders at their helm. So never look down upon your "small business." It is small now but has the potential to grow as long you embrace the right principles some are shared with you in this book.

After Samuel invited Saul to eat with him and be his guest he was amazed. The only thing is that he started remembering his smallness, the least of the tribes of Israel. Even within the tribes, the least of the families. This is dangerous. Later on, this is one of the reasons he felt threatened by David. We have a lot of people holding senior positions in organizations who feel threatened by the success and intelligence of their juniors. This attitude is always to the detriment of the business. Unfortunately many CEOs don't notice this. In fact it is difficult to detect.

Nevertheless Samuel didn't listen to his inferiority remarks and still invited him to eat with him. In fact Samuel asked of the portion of meat reserved for Saul, why? It is because God had a plan for Saul. When God has a plan for you, you will get divine favour and eat amongst the elite. Don't be amazed for too long because the meal with the elite is not the ultimate thing. The ultimate thing is kingship. Be amazed and thank God at the same time. You will surely eat with most renowned entrepreneurs and business people in this world. It is just a matter of time. You will be the first of firsts.

When things are tough, cry unto the Lord for He will hear you. God gave the Israelites a king that would save them from the hand of the Philistines because He had heard their cries (V16). Your cries to God will not be in vain. The reason why the children of Israel were freed from Egypt is because God had heard their cries. Then he tasked Moses to do the job. The Israelites were supposed to spend 400 years in Egypt but they spent 430 years, an additional 30 years (Exodus 12: 41). God sent Moses to deliver the Israelites only after He had heard their cries. They had started seeking and crying to God. They spent an additional 30 years because they had not cried to God. They were suffering but it became entrenched in their daily lives. The same when they wanted to be saved from the hand of the Philistines, they cried out to God and He heard their cries. He chose Saul. God will hear your cries when you earnestly seek him. It's time to say to Mr. or Mrs. Suffering, "enough is enough." Pray so that poverty and suffering should forget your address.

When you feel that all hope is lost, always remember the story of Saul how he lost his donkeys only to be anointed as the first king of Israel.

We need to trust God. He knows where the money is, where the clients are and where the customers are. We, in our naked eyes, might not see all these. Just put your trust in Him. The Unites States of America, a powerful nation, places its trust in God. At one time Peter was asked whether Jesus paid temple tax. Peter was told to go and fish, he was to take the first fish that came up. In its mouth he would find some money. Wow. Jesus knew where the money was. He still does. Even the fish obeyed him. You can fish all you want but it's difficult to succeed without divine intervention. Who put the money in the fish's mouth? If you are able to answer this question, you will know who put the customers and clients there.

Peter was a fisherman by profession. The Lord will use your talents to do great things. Peter, being a fisherman, there was no way he would have known that there was money in the mouth of the fish, without Jesus' instructions. Most of us rely on our own abilities but seem not see the light at the end of the tunnel. I can see good things coming your way. Don't over rely on your own abilities because what they can help you accomplish will be very limited. We all need divine favour to do great things.

Chapter 21

BACKGROUND OF SUFFERING

Many of our parents suffered. Not only our parents but bosses as well, co-workers, brothers, sisters, peers and a lot of others. Usually these people went through pains and hardships. When you become an entrepreneur and have had a painful background of say climbing the corporate ladder or coming from an impoverished background, the cardinal rule is: NEVER TAKE IT ON OTHER PEOPLE.

It is not necessarily that others were born lucky; they have simply been placed under your care by the Almighty God. I have seen bosses take it on their subordinates, just because they suffered before and would want you to go through the same process. To you bosses and entrepreneurs who do this "PLEASE STOP NOW". The mere fact that you suffered does not mean your subordinates should suffer as well.

It is often said that we are all on a scale of suffering but at different points. On a scale of 1 to 10, you may or might have been at 6, you may be surprised to find out that the person whom you are tormenting is at 7, partly caused by you. The problem with most of us is that we feel, on a scale of 1 to 10, that we are on 11. This is not true. We are all within the 1 to 10 scale. We are all human beings, we all have feelings. God could have made you and me a donkey, a cat, a dog, a zebra but no, He chose to make you and me human beings instead – made in heaven and assembled on earth. Therefore tormenting others was not the original plan of God for your life. Bondage is bitter.

You hear the bosses parrot to their subordinates that they reached where they are after 15 years or so and that they should do the same. They will tell you how people were cruel to them along the way, both their bosses and friends. Well, it's unfortunate that these things happened to them but they should not hold their employees and subordinates at ransom. This appears to be common with the baby boomers.

Young people cannot take this anymore. In my fifteen years of working, I have noticed this. My responses to the hardships from my peers in 1995, was different from the response of the young guys who started work in 2009. We could swallow the hardships back then and work on, not the young people of today. They are so tactful nowadays. They will calculate their options. Have you ever heard of the "quit but stay" mentality? You will be working with employees that quit a long time ago but are still working for you. All of a sudden you find productivity dwindling, net profits declining, and customer satisfaction waning. The young people of today are more complex and do not welcome suffering easily.

As an entrepreneur you should be aware of this. Sometimes we look very far yet the answers are right in front of us. Our education system is more left-brain oriented. Yet to survive and compete effectively you need the left brain, right brain and the subconscious to be working in harmony. The subconscious takes the larger portion of the brain. The reason I have mentioned this is that our school system has made us work towards the same answers. This tends to limit us to challenge facts.

Have you ever wondered why there are hardly any new inventions any more? Those who are inventing now go out of their ways to think outside the box. Surprisingly there are a lot of school dropouts who are doing well, "A" students working for "B" and "C" students. The issue is that answers are in front of us only that we like to infer too much.

As an entrepreneur you will do better and succeed if you do not subject your employees and partners to the same hardships you went through or are currently going through. A lot of entrepreneurs never "walk the talk". The law of impartation always applies. If one is talking to a group of people about measles and he has flue, what are they going to catch? The measles he is lecturing on or the flue that he has? That is how the law of impartation works it's not what you say that matters most, but what they do.

No body wants to suffer. We were not born to suffer. Therefore let's not make others suffer just because we suffered. Fellow entrepreneurs, let's sing a new song. Entrepreneurship is a win-win situation. All you need to apply are various principles of leverage, control, the power of association, the power of attraction, formation of strong nuclei, taking risks, having a passion, self-management, applying the law of compounding and so forth. There are a lot of ways we can attract money and be successful. It's high time we stopped frightening those whom we expect to push us to the next level.

This is very true and practical. Millions of people all over the world are victims of their employers' past. They should stop this and treat people as people. It is not that we should ignore the past. Let us remember the past, both good and bad. Let us ensure that our employees and partners do not go through the same hardships that we went through. Those involved in service and charity work for the good of all should be applauded. Try to make the world a better place.

You can't save everybody but the one or two people whom you influence positively can make a difference. Imagine if all the entrepreneurs were to make this positive change to one or two people, it would literally change millions of people's lives. It starts with you and your attitude. I applaud entrepreneurs that are active in assisting their communities.

Keep in mind that the rules of both labour and money have changed. There has been a metamorphosis therefore we should not be left behind. A lot of new businesses fail within the first year. The issues just mentioned are some of the reasons. Imagine a company with over 80% of their employees in the "quit but stay" mode. The entity is bound to fail.

Chapter 22

YOU CAN'T BE EVERYBODY'S FRIEND

This is an honest fact. This does not mean that you have to be unfriendly, it basically spells out the fact that some people will be displeased with your progress and dreams. Remember what happened to Joseph when he told his brothers about his dreams? They ended up hating him more than they did before. Joseph was already hated by his brothers because his father Jacob, Israel, loved him the most. Telling them that he dreamt something made them to hate him even more.

What is scary is that when he explained the dream to them, they hated him much more. Just think about the levels of hate. First it was hate, then hated more, then hated him much more. This was coming from a brother-to-brother relationship. Some people very close to you might be indignant about your vision. Therefore be careful who you talk to and confide in. This is very common in business as well as politics.

Have you ever wondered why some nations never move forward? As long as the levels of hate increase they will never move forward but will be ever dependent on aid from other countries. That hate should be changed to love, once love and fairness exist, you can harness the natural rich minerals and till the fruitful fields that God gave you.

A country can prosper because of the sum total of successful entrepreneurs. These entrepreneurs are in different fields from agriculture, mining, manufacturing, education and a lot more diverse areas. If the "pull him down" syndrome persists, there will be no moving forward. We can come up with brilliant business strategies but it will be difficult to implement them as long as the "pull him down" syndrome persists, even the "I will not sink alone" attitude, or "we are in this together" syndrome. As long as this persists, countries will find it difficult to come out of the poverty trap.

These problems occur not only at country leadership level but also at business leadership level, amongst employees, as well as family level just like Joseph and his brothers. To overcome this, it starts with you. As you read this book, please consider your ways because you can tomorrow be in the leadership of a country, a business, or family. The fact is that it starts with you, don't look around and wait for others to change their mindsets, you might be disappointed.

Others may steal your ideas and implement them because of their financial muscle. For your own information there are many people out there with a lot of money, some even take loans but have not the slightest idea what business to venture into in order to multiply their money. There are people who are just waiting to photocopy your ideas.

Chapter 23

SACRIFICE

This is not an easy word. It sends shivers down my spine. Although a tough word to chew, it can lead to your breakthrough in business. There is a banker who sold his only house to finance his dream of opening a bank. Right now he is successful beyond measure. Good things don't come cheap or easy. There is high level of sacrifice involved.

My wife and I had two heaters in our home that we had not really been making full use of. In one year it was really cold. The cold season could send you gnashing your teeth. Now there were monthly sales that our church was conducting to mobilize resources in the church. The church was asking for people to bring in items they are not using in their homes so that they could put them up for sale. Guess what we did. We gave those two heaters to the church. At first I hesitated because that was when we needed the heaters most during the cold season. That is what I call sacrifice. We sowed a seed. When you sow you expect to reap. So we prayed to God and asked what we needed in our lives.

Have you ever heard of tithing? Yes, that 10% of your gross income should be paid as tithe. A lot of my friends were tithing except me. I could see them being promoted at work, business deals coming in, a lot of things were happening. It is because they were sacrificing 10% of their income. Some ask whether you should tithe 10% of gross income or 10% of net income. One subtly put it that when you give 10% of gross income or gross profit, you receive gross blessings. If you give 10% of net income or net profit, you will receive net blessings.

There is a story that is told concerning tithing. There was a certain old lady who used to give 90% of her income and live on only 10%. One day when listening to a sermon on tithing she realized that she was supposed to be giving 10% and not 90%. By then the Lord had blessed her with so much. Those are the fruits of sacrifice.

If you cannot fund your own dreams then it's asking for too much for others to fund them.

At least part-fund them by scarifying your time to plan ahead. Sacrifice needs not only be in notes and coins. With notes and coins you can leverage your money.

This brings me to the point of, "THE BIG SIN". Each of us struggles with 'the big sin'. There is one big sin that we seem not to let go of. That big, single sin holds us captive. As you start your entrepreneurial venture you need to let go. Sacrifice the big sin. I suppose something is going through your mind right now. Yes that one, you need to let go. If you are heading for success the big sin will end up being excess baggage.

When you start a business, your mind has to be as light as possible. This will ensure that you absorb fresh ideas that will usher you forward and upward. Excess baggage will bring you down before you even start. That is why sacrifice is very difficult indeed. We have our own stories to tell of people who sacrificed a lot to support their dreams.

Some people sacrifice sleep for a reasonable period just to ensure they start well. Never listen to those people who say that they will not lose sleep over this and that. What prompted them to say that is the fact that they are actually losing sleep.

Sacrifice and giving go hand in hand. As an entrepreneur also learn to give materially, giving of your abundance. I have met friends and religious people who, when you give indications that you need material assistance, will start giving you "good" advice. They will tell you about "10 ways of getting out of debt", "10 ways of living a happier life", "10 ways of staying out of trouble", "10 ways of this and that". All you need at that time was some money for bus fare or fuel for your car or some assistance with school fees, or money to buy some food. Let's be quick readers of other people's needs and act accordingly.

God has blessed us with so much, including material things. This is very true, one day I was trying to partly pay off a nagging debt I had. After explaining the issue to a friend, I got a lecture on the different ways of how one gets into debt. At that time some notes and coins would have been more effective than a lecture. Some people present issues to us not to lecture them but to assist them financially. Once you bless others as an entrepreneur you will receive back in abundance. God will hear the prayers of that person you have given. Once that person prays to the Lord, after meeting the conditions of a prayer to be heard, to bless you, He will surely bless you.

Chapter 24

LIFE IS LIKE A PARADOX

Life is like a paradox, the more you think you are enjoying yourself the more you waste yourself. A lot of people are involved in pleasure binges and think that is what life is all about. Despite all the dangers and risks attached to "fun" people never seem to stop. Even if you advise people that they are wasting an important resource, time, they never listen. A lot of entrepreneurs instead of spending valuable time planning ahead, they rather "enjoy" themselves. It's called taking a short break.

There are entrepreneurs who are involved in a pleasurable life and those that take it easy. The outgoing and pleasurable entrepreneurs are always under various pressures. They are under pressure of sourcing money, time, decision-making and so forth. The steady ones are cool and shrewd because they have already planned ahead.

The paradox in business is balancing between profitability and cash flows. You might be very profitable but have cash problems. To me this is one of the biggest challenges for the entrepreneur. You have to make the entity both profitable and have sound net cash inflows on an ongoing basis. Whatever your business venture is, always ensure that it is sustainable. Ask yourself, "is this sustainable?" Remember that for every action one takes there is always a cost attached. I never wanted to admit to this notion but look at it closely. Just try today, even on social issues.

Every decision you make even to be a friend of someone there is a cost attached. As an entrepreneur, you should be conscious that for every business and social decisions you make, there is a hidden cost attached to it.

Bear in mind always that we are living in a world of awesome progress but paradoxically also one of appalling evils. What might seem as progress in your eyes might not necessarily usher you to your next level. Don't only strive to move forward but also upwards.

Chapter 25

AS BUSY AS A BEE

At primary school, 3rd to 7th Grade, we had an afternoon Christian group called Busy Bee. God may you bless Mrs Baisley, my primary school teacher then. She was a wonderful teacher, a teacher with love and compassion. I always hope and trust that we have teachers of her quality. My classmates from 1984 – 1988 would agree with me. I only met her once in 1998 and I pray that I will see her again soon to thank her for her beautiful heart. This lady in 1984 used to take the whole class for ice cream at her own expense. How many teachers still do this today without knocking at the school bursar's office?

Never be idle. An idle mind is the devil's workshop. Be as busy as a bee. Fill up your time with some positive things to do. If you don't, the bad things will start occupying your time. Being busy does not only mean studying for an exam. When you hear some people saying, "I am very busy these days", most of them are busy with their studies. Being busy can be reading business magazines, writing a book, participating in church events, doing charity work or looking after children. As an entrepreneur you have to be as busy as a bee. Find something to do. I have resolved to fill up my diary by doing service or charity work plus writing. Hard work is prayer in action.

Some employees only work during normal working hours at low levels of productivity, may be three hours for an eight hour pay day. Wow. When you work, work like a bee. A lot of people will look at you and ask you whether you own the company or firm. Those are the lazy guys. Just continue working hard, somebody is watching you. God is always watching. In addition to this, there are people watching you as well. People who wish you well, people who would want to have an employee like you, people who would want to have a business partner like you.

There is always someone watching you, even if you don't see them, continue working hard. If you are a lady, work as hard as you can. Some entities are looking for assertive women like you. After always working long hours thinking that no one was noticing, brought misery in my life, I complained to a friend who encouraged me to continue working hard, assuring me that with hard work, someone would eventually notice it. Remember, your miracle is in your assignment.

Your immediate boss might not notice you but someone else will. You were not made to work for that boss for the rest of your life. Continue working hard. Work as if you have been tipped for a promotion. Even if your boss shouts at you from time to time, continue working hard, as busy as a bee. Remember you were not created to work for that boss for the rest of your life. It is true that the greater the heat in the furnace the purer the gold. You remember Shadrach, Meshach and Abed-Nego. They were put in a burning fiery furnace. Nebuchadnezzar gave instructions to make the furnace exceedingly hot such that the flame of the fire killed those men that took the three into that furnace.

Even when you can't stand the heat, continue being as busy as a bee, instead of trying to get out of the kitchen.

Being busy does not automatically make you rich or successful but prepares you for greatness. Young David was always busy attending to his sheep, fighting bears and lions. This did not immediately make him king or head shepherd but it prepared him for future success and greatness. When you think no one is watching you, think again.

Peter, Andrew, James and John were fishermen. These were the first four disciples called by Jesus. They were called whilst working. They were busy bees. Peter and Andrew were casting a net into the sea, James and John were mending their nets. The four were not basking in the sun, no, they were busy working. Elisha who succeeded Elijah as a prophet was ploughing with twelve yokes of oxen when Elijah first approached him. A lot of people pray and don't work and expect blessings to come their way, but this is not so. Your miracle is in your assignment. You have to work. Don't leave room for idleness to creep into your life, work hard, harder, hardest.

Our God is a God that works as well. He is a working God. It is recorded in Genesis that the earth was without form. God worked from day one to day seven. He still works in our lives. Your business can be without form and you need to work on it with God's help. God expects you to work. You have to be as busy as a bee.

Teach your employees, business partners, families, children, friends to be as busy as bees. In the case of a firm or enterprise, you are guaranteed of increased turnover. The rest is obvious.

Chapter 26

WHO WILL TEACH OUR CHILDREN?

Who will teach our children entrepreneurial skills at a tender age? Entrepreneurial skills need to be inculcated into the young ones at tender ages. It is up to us to teach the younger ones. A good man leaves inheritance for his children's children. If we embrace this thought, discipline will be instilled in our business lives. Never run away from the pain of discipline otherwise the pain of regret will haunt you. A good or real man does not fight for inheritance but leaves inheritance.

Practical skills subjects should be aggressively promoted. It seems the service sector is getting saturated. We need people who create wealth.

In 1988 when I was in the 7th grade one of our teachers taught us practical craft skills. Of particular interest to me was making vase holders out of strings. Students would make beautiful vase holders, competitions would be held to encourage creativity. It was interesting to learn from those who made superb vase holders. Unfortunately in the years to come, I never developed the skill. Only my 7th grade teacher told us the importance of such skills. He stressed that not all of us would be in the service industry therefore we had to learn hands-on skills. I heard him but did not take it serious as i believed that that sort of life was not for me.

Only 17 years later did I see the opportunity presented by many homes being without string vase holders. This I felt I could do it part time to supplement my income. I was seeing what other people were not seeing. I tried to buy some strings and tried the skills, I learnt earlier but was unsuccessful. After a few months, I decided to visit my 1988 teacher after 17 years. By this time I was working in a different country. He was many miles away. My spirits sunk low when I heard that he had passed away. This was a double blow to me as I felt guilty for not ever visiting him during the years and for not putting into practice the skills he taught us. Perhaps if he had approached it from a different angle, maybe I would have listened and absorbed it better. Most of the times 'A' students shun practical subjects. There I was with a business opportunity but did not have the skills to implement it. I trust that one day I will venture into this area. Remember, life is very unpleasant for quitters.

Chapter 27

BEWARE OF "FIRST" CUSTOMERS OR CLIENTS

The earliest bird catches the fattest worm. You have to be on your guard for "first" customers or clients. They definitely know your capabilities and some would want to offer themselves as "first" customers / clients. These customers or clients could have known you from your previous employers and might have even offered you a job at one point. They will definitely place an order for your stocks but will demand a ridiculously low price and at the same time negotiate extended credit terms.

Be very careful, it will cost you a lot chasing that money. Instead of investing your time to procure more stocks or do some planning, you might end up doing unnecessary debt collection trips. The same applies to consulting work, the first stage of the consultancy process is entry, then diagnosis. Some of the "first" clients will ask you to diagnose a problem for free. They will tell you to start charging once you start the action planning or problem solving stage. The unfortunate thing about this arrangement is that time is money.

As a consultant you have a charge-out rate that has to be met whether you are diagnosing a problem or solving one. The "firsts" can really be a problem. There is no harm in being selective. Try to find out the cash flows of your first customers or clients. You need to have some professional scepticism. Take reasonable risk without being over excited of securing your first customers or clients. Have the courage to say no to a prospect. It will save you a lot; it may end up saving your new business.

This is the time when you should rely on your cash-rich contacts. Look around you, see the people you interact with, that is you in five years' time. It is good to form a strong nucleus of friends, of varied socio-economic backgrounds. These are the people who will push you up. Interact with these people of different professions and interests to yours. You will learn a lot from them. Sometimes they might not give you hard cash but an opportunity. Grab whatever you can get. They have cash rich friends whom they can refer you to. That is the advantage of having a wide web of friends. Try to keep quality relationships that are symbiotic. They should also ask you questions in which you are well versed. In that way they will respect you as well. These friends and their contacts can safely be part of your first customers or clients.

Chapter 28

PERSONAL AUDIT

This is a process whereby you look at your own life from the time you were born till now. The time you were born refers to the time as far back as you can remember.

I receive a lot of calls and attend meetings where people ask me what they can profitably venture into. This is a very difficult question to answer. As I write someone called me this morning saying that she had capital but needed my advice as to what business to venture. It was very difficult to answer immediately but assured her that I would think of something.

There is good reason for bringing up this issue of a personal audit. It is for the simple reason that millions of people have raised capital but simply don't know what to venture into. This is part of the solution to would-be callers and those facing a similar situation.

It has been revealed that more than 80% of a child's creativity is lost by the age of fifteen, if that creative ability is not nurtured. A lot of people have influenced our lives over the years, some positively, others negatively. Look back from the time you were born, as far back as you can remember. What talents did you show that were never nurtured? What positive things did your primary school and high school teachers tell you about your future? What sports did you excel in? Were you good in craft or practical skills? What school club did you belong to? There must be something you were good at.

A lot of people mainly bosses have no time to ask you these questions. You only have to add value to the organization. Once you start asking yourself these questions, you will discover your suppressed skills. You will clearly see what business venture you can pursue. Many people have lied to us that we can't make it. They have set "untouchable qualifications" by which we have automatically disqualified ourselves. You may not be a good "numbers" person but could be very artistic. The major problem with a lot of us is that we do not want to explore, for fear of failure. The fear mainly stems from the effort one would have gone through to obtain the start up capital or the sacrifices undertaken to even start.

I don't believe in TNT, Truly No Talent. The talent is there somewhere. Do a personal audit and you will discover your talent. Go somewhere very quiet and close your eyes and look back. You will not be able to do this in one day but can take a week or two to open all the pages of your past.

After some deep search, it dawned on me that I had a talent that was not nurtured. That is writing. The personal audit was done during some tough times. No matter how much I worked hard, one of the bosses would go bananas. It made me to think whether I had a problem or not. Other employers were willing to pay me twice what I was gettingIt made me think. It made me think bigger than big.

It meant going through the life I had with my parents, and analyzing what positive things they said about me. I also went through my pre-school, high school and college years – the church life I had and all the teachers who had great influence on me. In primary school, I was the best swimmer in a particular year. Good tennis player in secondary. During my secondary school years, I was made tuck-shop man, school prefect, sports writer, chairman of the debating club, chairman of the scripture union, class monitor, house captain, teacher of Sunday school children, editor of the school magazine. What did the teachers and fellow students see in me? I was always called upon to do impromptu speeches, especially vote of thanks to school visitors. I was a leader. All these people saw leadership skills in me. Unfortunately I did not develop my leadership skills. I even tried later on to duck and dive when given leadership roles.

Whatever the negative attitude a boss had, was all wrong. The problem is that some people are good at suppressing other peoples' talents. Beware to talent oppressors (TOs).

People ask whether a leader is born or made. I believe a leader is made, with the exception of Moses. Once a leader is made, it is difficult to break him/her. That unbreakable quality is the one that makes people believe that a leader is born, that tenacity.

In our 1992 school magazine, I wrote an article and three poems. Till now, I remember them and what motivated me to write them. One day I would love to get hold of the 1992 school magazine and read them out to a wide audience. Those were masterpiece poems.

Being the school's sports writer made me write tantalizing reports. One of my teachers from Canada was shocked at the excellent quality of my essays. My fellow schoolmates will attest to this.

Eventually I pursed numbers as a career and parked my talent in writing. When I talk to people it seems I never run out of what to say, at least. My father, Bruce, gave me good advice "When you have nothing to say, keep quiet". So I only talk when I have a meaningful contribution. My writing skills were developed at that youthful age. This is why I decided to write this book. A combination of what I used to do fifteen years ago and life and business experiences.

You too can do a personal audit of your life. Be very critical of yourself. Only portraying a rosy picture will not do. A lot of people are described as "Not a people person." Maybe you excelled in individual sports than team sports.

The negative things that people say about you, is completely false. A lot of people venture into business that they have no clue about, only because there is a lot of cash there. Do something you have a passion for. You are the best in that area. If cash is your game then consider investments. If it's marketing, then go for it. Never believe the bad things that other people say about you.

You might have pursued a particular career, I am not encouraging you to stop. I am encouraging you to augment your earnings, to know what business venture to go into once you have capital, a venture that best matches your talent. To parents, let's aim at developing our children's creative abilities. Do your own personal audit and you will find the hidden answers.

Chapter 29

CELEBRATE YOUR VICTORY IN ADVANCE

Hold on to your dream, everyday act and think as if you have achieved your goals. Celebrate in advance. This will ensure that you will not take your eyes off the ball. Walk like a victor, act like a victor. This will release positive energies in you. Even if you have financial or emotional problems, by holding onto your dream, the problems will not break you because you have already believed that you are a victor.

It bothers others sometimes when you are radiant or walk like a champion. Walk confidently, talk confidently. Your voice projection, body language, eye contact, handshake should confirm that you are a victor. As an entrepreneur you find people come closer to you asking you for ideas. Profitably they will ask you to supply some of your products or services. There are very few people out there who radiate victory. In fact victory should be your middle name.

Larry Bird said 'a winner is someone who recognizes his God-given talents, works his tail off to develop them into skills and uses these skills to accomplish his goals.' You too can be a winner.

We all are sceptical of people at first or second contacts. This also applies to prospective customers or clients. Unfortunately the mastery of this concept has fallen into the wrong hands. Have you ever noticed that some people are excellent in job interviews but when given the actual job to do they fail dismally? These people have mastered the art of victorious living. When in the interview they already see themselves as working.

A friend taught me how to communicate confidence and tickle the interviewing panel's fancy. He said that when the interview has come to an end, thank them and say, "I hope the next time we meet we will meet as workmates." This is great and powerful confidence. You can also be this confident. That will be your competitive advantage. There is a lot of competition out there as much as there are many businesses.

You don't have to go far to have a competitive advantage over the highly educated crew.

When you celebrate your victory people will think that you are rich. Anyway that is where you are going, abundant riches and success. If there are setbacks in the process, take them as minor, your attitude is key to how fast you recover. You are the only one who can amplify these vicissitudes of life. Victorious living has no room for unending weeping.

It is important to start doing something, knowing that you will be a victor. If you want to venture into entrepreneurship – JUST START. You can't live a victorious life without doing or starting anything. A journey of a thousand miles starts with a single step.

I am already celebrating the success of this book as I contribute to making the world a better place.

Chapter 30

RICH SAYINGS

The sayings below should guide you in analyzing situations, events and people.

(i) Tears don't wipe away sins.

I have seen a lot of crocodile tears in my lifetime. The mere fact that you make noisy cries, does not necessarily tantamount to cancellation of the bad deed. Repentance is better than crying. This is very common at funerals, people cry a lot but to find out what good they contributed to the life of the deceased, you will find that the answer is "none". Maybe they are tears of regret.

From a business perspective, do your best to attend a short course on risk management. This will reduce the likelihood of shading business-related tears.

(ii) You can't destroy a bad habit by cultivating another one.

Do your best to develop best business practices.

(Songs of Solomon 2: 15) says: "Catch for us the foxes, the little foxes that ruin the vineyards, our vineyards that are in boom"

May these little foxes or habits not bring your business down. You have to give up some old habits that don't add value to your life and business. Getting rid of the old bad habits is not enough if you go on developing new bad habits.

(iii) We are on the verge of a stupendous crisis.

(iv) We are living in a world of awesome progress but paradoxically one of appalling evil.

(v) A thing of beauty is a joy forever.

(vi) Never argue with a fool otherwise people will not notice the difference.

Engage in constructive conversations. I love business conversations. When people converse on issues of the economy, money, entrepreneurship and alike, I always, in one way or the other, want to be part of them. You will be amazed how much you can learn.

Avoid unnecessary debates. As an entrepreneur you should not have time for this. Do something else. If there isn't much to do, it's better to take a nap and relax.

(vii) Life is like peeling a lemon, sometimes you cry.

When you cry, you should not over do it. Sorrow dims one's vision. You might fail to look ahead because you are wasting time weeping. In (1 Samuel 16: 1), the Lord said to Samuel: "How long will you mourn for Saul, since I have rejected him as king of Israel? ..."

(viii) A good man leaves inheritance for his children's children.

Don't think of yourself only as you go about building your business. Also focus on others. Think of how your actions today as a father, mother, entrepreneur, President, Prime Minister, church leader will impact on the generations to come. It is sad to read in the newspapers of people fighting over their father's wealth, instead of creating their own and leaving it for their children's children. Look closely into your value goals as you go about doing your business.

Inheritance is both spiritual inheritance and inheritance of wealth.

(ix) Laughter is medicine

Sometime ago I used to see in job vacancy adverts in newspapers, that one of the requirements of the person sought was a high sense of humour. Your prospects of getting the job would be very low, if you had no sense of humour.

I encourage companies to put this as one of the requirements when recruiting employees, especially for high level positions.

Don't go about as if you are chewing some lemon. Laugh with others, you will be amazed what laughter can do to one's pocket.

Why do you think Kings had jesters? They knew the power of laughter.

(x)   If you sow the wind, you will reap the whirlwind.

This is true. If you engage in useless and non-value adding activities you will not accomplish anything worthwhile. Always aim at engaging in something productive for your own good and for the good of others.

INDEX

A

Abed-Nego, 120
African dream, ix
Amalekites, 21, 97
Angel of God, 3
Animal husbandry, 16

B

Benchmarking, 71, 72
Busy Bee, 119

C

Caleb, 30
Canaan, 30
Canada, 129
Cash flows, 37, 97
Chicago Academy of Fine Arts, 5
Club Aluminium, 92
constructive criticism, 58
Covenant University, 7

D

Daniel, 11, 22, 23, 31
Decision Making Unit, 63
Deuteronomy, 45
Disneyland, 6
dominant or major gift, 12, 15

E

Egypt, 3, 13, 14, 15, 16, 23, 24, 30, 43, 72, 105
Eliab, 20, 99
Elijah, 8, 25, 44, 120
Elisha, 8, 11, 25, 95, 96, 120
Esau, 7
Exodus, 3, 24, 43, 105

F

Flawed Desires + Temptation = Sin, 47
Florida, 6

G

Ghana, 10
Goliath, 18, 20, 21
Good Samaritan, 33, 34
Gossip, 57
GP value per unit, 69

H

Humility, 95, 96

I

Ishmaelites, 14, 16
Israel, 3, 16, 18, 19, 20, 21, 23, 24, 30, 43, 67, 96, 97, 99, 101, 102, 104, 105, 111, 134

J

Jesus, 9, 47, 58, 103, 105, 106, 120
Joseph, 11, 12, 13, 14, 15, 16, 20, 23, 31, 111, 112
Joshua, 30

K

Keliah, 16
King Belshazzar, 23
KISS, 52

L

Los Angeles, 6
Luke, 47

M

Malawi, 54
Mandela, Nelson, 8
Matthew, 3, 9, 58
Mephibosheth, 16
Meshach, 120
Mickey Mouse, 5, 7
Money, 37, 39
Mortimer Mouse, 7
Moses, 11, 23, 24, 30, 43, 105, 128
Mother Theresa, 74
Mount Sinai, 24
Mulanje, 54

N

Namaan, 95, 96
Nebuchadnezzar, 120

O

Oswald the rabbit, 5, 6
Oyedepo, Dr David, 7, 29

P

Peter, 9, 105, 106, 120
Pharaoh, 3, 13, 14, 15, 23
Philistines, 3, 16, 102, 105
Positive thinking, 33, 34
Promised Land, 23, 31
Proverbs, 3, 87
Psalms, 17
pull him down syndromes, 38

R

Red Sea, 24
River Jordan, 25, 96
Romans, 13, 43, 91

S

Sacrifice, 113, 114
Samuel, 16, 19, 97, 99, 101, 102, 104, 105, 134
Satan, 47
Saul, 18, 19, 21, 96, 97, 101, 102, 103, 104, 105, 134
Shadrach, 120
shallow foundation, 11
SMART, 52
South Africa, 8
Southern Africa, 85
successful entrepreneur, x, 19, 21, 91

T

Test of Three Cups', 92

Index

V

vision, ix, 1, 2, 3, 4, 5, 6, 7, 8, 9, 10, 19, 29, 31, 65, 66, 77, 111, 134

W

Walt Disney, 4, 5, 6, 31

Y

Yahweh-Yireh, 9

Z

Ziklag, 21

www.ingramcontent.com/pod-product-compliance
Lightning Source LLC
Chambersburg PA
CBHW071331190426
43193CB00041B/1485